Special
Operations
Forces

SPECIAL OPERATIONS FORCES

An Assessment

John M. Collins

National Defense University Press
Washington, DC

National Defense University Press Publications

To increase general knowledge and inform discussion, the Institute for National Strategic Studies, through its publication arm the NDU Press, publishes McNair Papers; proceedings of University- and Institute-sponsored symposia; books relating to U.S. national security, especially to issues of joint, combined, or coalition warfare, peacekeeping operations, and national strategy; and a variety of briefer works designed to circulate contemporary comment and offer alternatives to current policy. The Press occasionally publishes out-of-print defense classics, historical works, and other especially timely or distinguished writing on national security.

NDU Press publications are sold by the U.S. Government Printing Office. For ordering information, call (202) 783-3238 or write to the Superintendent of Documents, US Government Printing Office, Washington, DC 20402.

Library of Congress Cataloguing in Publication Data

Collins, John M., 1921–
    Special operations forces: as assessment, 1986-1993 / John M. Collins.
        p. cm.
    Includes bibliographical references and index.
    1. Special forces (Military science)—United States—Evaluation.
    I. Title.
U262.C647   1994
356'.16'0973—dc20   94-8981
                                           CIP

First printing, April 1994

To U.S. Special Operations Forces

They who do more with less

They who proudly accept the most difficult and dangerous missions in their service to the Nation

They who frequently lay the supreme sacrifice on the altar of freedom

Contents

Figures

Tables

Photographs

Foreword

The end of the Cold War and severe reductions in the defense budget might appear to argue against preserving military groups outside the standard force structure. We are learning the very opposite, however. As global politics turn regional, the value of Special Operations Forces (SOF) is becoming increasingly important.

Future crises will require regional orientation, language proficiency, and rapid response—all things for which SOF are trained—and for less than 1 percent of the defense budget. To help determine whether SOF are necessary and cost-effective, Chairman Sam Nunn and Senator William Cohen of the Senate Armed Services Committee asked the Congressional Research Service's senior military analyst John Collins to assess the capabilities and contributions of the Special Operations Forces. This book is an enlargement and extension of Mr. Collins' original report, further enriched by dramatic and illuminating illustrations.

Although no policy recommendations are presented, the careful reader may discern the value of SOF and the gains to be achieved by their unique training. The author views these special forces as neither superfluous nor elite in a world where military challenges and requirements are no longer "standard." Written after exhaustive research throughout the SOF community and with open access across the board, this book represents the most thorough assessment of Special Operations Forces currently in print.

PAUL G. CERJAN
Lieutenant General, U.S. Army
President, National Defense University

Introduction

In this volume, John Collins speaks with the authority of one who was literally present at the birth of the "low intensity conflict" era. His long-term, intimate, and direct contact with the esoteric world of special operations has few parallels.

Their roots go back in time and history considerably farther, but today's Special Operations Forces are largely products of the past three decades. Their development has been in response to the pressures of world-wide situations perceived to bear upon or which actually do affect American strategic interests. The use of raw military power may not provide solutions to the complex problems involved and may even be counter-productive. Special Operations Forces, uniquely suited to fill the quasi-military gap, require the highest degree of professional competence in the application of the classical principles of war. This is a big order.

It is difficult in a few words to pay John Collins the tribute he deserves for continuing efforts to educate both the Congress and the U.S. Armed Forces concerning the capabilities and limitations of special operations and the forces they involve. This latest addition to his carefully researched studies combines history, philosophy, factual data, and reference materials in a single document that should be on the desks of civilian and military leaders whose responsibilities relate in any way to special operations.

William P. Yarborough
Lieutenant General, USA (Ret)

Lieutenant General Yarborough served in many commands during his illustrious career but is perhaps best known for being Commanding General of the U.S. Army Special Warfare Center from 1961 to 1965. It was during this tenure that President Kennedy's personal interest made the Green Berets world famous. An icon for Special Operations Forces, General Yarborough served several years as a member of the Special Operations Policy Advisory Group. It is an interesting historical note that he designed the Army paratrooper wings, jump suit, and jump boots used during WWII, then made four combat jumps, two in Algeria, one in Sicily, and one in southern France.

Acknowledgments

This report was made possible when General Carl W. Stiner, in his capacity as Commander-in-Chief of United States Special Operations Command (USSOCOM), pledged full cooperation and told all four component commanders to do likewise. His personal involvement set a precedent. Lieutenant General Wayne A. Downing explained the status of U.S. Army Special Operations Command (USASOC) in a free-flowing discussion that lasted 3 hours, arranged displays, and provided documents. Rear Admiral Raymond C. Smith hosted a lengthy orientation at Naval Special Warfare Command (NAVSPECWARCOM). The Deputy Commanders of U.S. Air Force Special Operation Command (AFSOC) and Joint Special Operations Command (JSOC) did likewise in the absence of Major Generals Bruce L. Fister and William Garrison. General Colin L. Powell, Chairman of the Joint Chiefs of Staff, secured the cooperation of the the five regionally oriented Commanders in Chief to assist in the preparation of this report. Admiral Paul David Miller, whose Atlantic Command headquarters is close to Washington, D.C., personally described plans for closer connections between special operations and conventional forces.

Perhaps 200 staff officers reviewed the first draft. Many of them expressed opinions at roundtable discussions. Experienced retirees, colleagues in the Congressional Research Service, and free-lance specialists also furnished facts and interpretations. I salute them all, but was able to identify by name only those cited below.

Panoramic and service-specific views came from the Pentagon. Captain John Sandoz (USN), Chris Lamb, and Tom Myerchin were sources in the Office of the Assistant Secretary of Defense for Special Operations and Low-Intensity Conflict. Colonel James Kraus, Lieutenant Colonels Glenn Harned and Bob Huckabee (all USA), Commander Walt Pullar, and Major John Pryor (USAF) were points of contact on the Joint Staff (J-3 Special Operations Division). Lieutenant Colonel Greg Jones; Commander Bill Cheatham; Lieutenant Colonels Bernie Moore and Ray Killgore; and Colonel Chandler Crangle represented the U.S. Army, Navy, Air Force, and Marine Corps respectively.

The USSOCOM staff furnished professional assistance throughout the production process. Flag officers included Rear Admiral Irve C. LeMoyne, now Deputy Commander-in-Chief, Major General James A. Guest (USA), and Major General James C. McComb (USAF). Marine Lieutenant Colonel Gregg Turner, my main contact for almost four months, fielded requests for information, arranged for reviews, and escorted my week-long tour of USSOCOM's facilities. Seven other officers represented USSOCOM J-5 (Policies, Plans, and Doctrine): Captain Paul Shemella, USN; Colonels Corky Hilton and James Townsend (USA); Lieutenant Colonels Sal Cambria and Ronnie Rhoads (USA); Commander Bob Harger; and Major John Hill (USAF). Lieutenant Commander Anne Jewell spoke for the J-1 (Personnel), Colonel Paul Morgan (USA) and Warrent Bradish for J-2 (Intelligence). Colonel Eugene Bernhardt and Major Bill Burgess (both USA) offered perspectives from J-3 (Operations). Gary Smith, the Deputy for Acquisition, together with Colonels Robert Bayless (USAF) and David Merriam (USA), helped with logistics. Colonel John Donnelly and Lieutenant Colonel Peter Atherton (USA) focused on civil affairs and psychological operations. Lieutenant Colonels Edmund Davis (USA), Chester Morgan (USAF) and Dr. John Partin provided medical, legal, and historical advice. Captain Tom Quigley (USN) and Major John Mol (USAF) in USSOCOM's Washington Office backstopped Greg Turner from start to finish. Lieutenant Colonel Dave Maki also filled many blank spots. Margaret Kinkead was a budgetary whiz.

Staff officers who devoted a lot of time and attention at USSOCOM's component commands included Colonel Darnell Katz and Major Harry Stryffeler at USASOC; Colonel Lee Hess, Lieutenant Colonels Charles Williamson, Bo Tye, and Maggie Timmons at AFSOC; Captain Tim Holden and Commodore Joe Quincannon at NAVSPECWARCOM. Captain James Sherlock (USN), Colonel Travis Griffin, and Lieutenant Colonel James Velky (both USA), represented LANTCOM and SOCLANT. Their counterparts in other unified commands were Colonel Tom Smith, Lieutenant Colonels Sid Morgan (USA) and Clark Lee (USAF), Major Mac McCausland (USAF), and Lieutenant Commander Tucker Campion, CENTCOM/SOCCENT; Lieutenant Colonel Michael Dredla (USAF), PACOM and Lieutenant Commander Alfred Artho, SOCPAC; Lieutenant Colonel Jim McGarrach (USA), EUCOM/SOCEUR; Lieutenant Colonel Charles Zimmerman (USA) and Lieutenant Colonel, J.D. Cameron (USAF),

SOUTHCOM/SOCSOUTH; and Colonel Skip Booth (USA), SOC-KOREA.

Mentors in the retired community with a wealth of special operations experience and/or "insider" know-how were General Bob Kingston, Lieutenant Generals Sam Wilson and Dick Trefry (all USA), Brigadier General Walter Jajko (USAF), and five colonels; Ed Abood, Gene Russell, Scot Crerar, and Peter Bahnsen (USA), and John Roberts (USAF). Mark Lowenthal, Bob Goldich, Jim Wootten, and Ted Galdi were sounding boards within the Congressional Research Service.

Barbara Hennix typed most of my handwritten draft and patiently inserted countless corrections. Dianne Rennack, my junior partner for several years, was an unbeatable backup when deadlines drew near. Swift, my spouse, kept me fed, clothed, and reassured throughout the stressful gestation of this report. I could not do well without her help.

John M. Collins

Preface

> One cannot get effectiveness without paying a cost. The way to
> get the most effective total defense program is to try to put each
> dollar where it will add the most to total effectiveness. The
> emphasis is not on cost, but on cost *and* effectiveness together.
>
> *Alain C. Enthoven and K. Wayne Smith,*
> How Much Is Enough?

Current plans call for the smallest U.S. military establishment since
the Korean War ended 40 years ago, and it may be difficult to
maintain even the remainder at present high standards, because the
planned results of this austere defense budget could prove overly
optimistic. Recruiters already must work harder to enlist first-rate
young men and women for a military career that offers fewer
opportunities than during the Cold War. More than ever, the
Department of Defense needs to extract maximum value from every
dollar, so each program is being closely examined, including Special
Operations Forces (SOF).

SOF comprised less than 2 percent of the U.S. armed forces and
consumed slightly more than 1 percent of the defense budget at the
end of Fiscal Year 1993. Their mission was well summed up by
General Carl W. Stiner, when he was Commander in Chief of the
U.S. Special Operations Command (USSOCOM). He found SOF
ideal to cope with "the types of crises we will most likely face in the
future. That future will require the regional orientation, cultural
awareness, language proficiency, and quick responsiveness which
very often make SOF the force of choice in an increasingly unstable
world. Those capabilities have resulted from more than five years of
training—as a team, at every level—to demanding combat standards
under a single command with its own program and budget...Our
priority should be not only to maintain this team, but to continue to
improve it."[1]

Some senior officials in the Pentagon seem unconvinced.
Secretary of Defense Les Aspin originally planned to have the
Assistant Secretary of Defense for Special Operations and Low-
Intensity Conflict (ASD SO/LIC) report to another ASD rather than
the Under Secretary for Policy. No U.S. service chief obviously

favors special operations during this period of force reductions and budgetary constraints, and the SOF constituency on Capitol Hill and in industry is quite small. Moreover, negative and neutral views of SOF are common at lower levels throughout the U.S. military establishment. Critics complain that SOF not only require different command/control arrangements (sometimes directly to National Command Authorities), weapons, equipment, training, intelligence support, and funding than conventional forces they supplant, complement, or supplement, but also divert many first-rate officers and noncommissioned officers from Army, Navy, and Air Force units. They doubt that SOF are worth the effort.

This report was prepared at the request of Chairman Sam Nunn and Senator William Cohen of the Senate Armed Services Committee (see appendix A) to help Congress assess the current and future capabilities of SOF, with particular attention to personnel, equipment, and budgetary requirements in the post-Cold War world. It summarizes special operations problems before Congress enacted corrective legislation in 1986-87-88, reviews subsequent progress, and identifies residual problems and options that might maintain and improve SOF performance (appendix B, General Stiner's *End of Tour Report*, assesses the situation from a different perspective).[2]

Information came from rich sources such as official documents, briefings, and informal discussions; demonstrations in the Pentagon and at Headquarters USSOCOM and its component commands; and regionally oriented U.S. unified commands. Knowledgeable individuals furnished additional facts and opinions. Comments from a wide variety of reviewers refined the first draft.

These assessments, prepared in conformance with Congressional Research Service guidelines, present no policy recommendations. Readers must decide for themselves whether the capabilities that U.S. Special Operations Forces offer dovetail with conventional military power to provide maximum effectiveness at optimum cost.

Notes

1. General Carl W. Stiner, *Memorandum for the Chairman of the Joint Chiefs of Staff, Subject: CJCS Roles and Missions Report* (MacDill AFB, FL: Hq. USSOCOM, 1993), 3.

2. For a complementary review of U.S. Special Operations Forces, see Douglas C. Waller, *The Commandos: The Inside Story of America's Secret Soldiers* (New York: Simon & Schuster, 1994).

Special
Operations
Forces

I. Special Operations Specialties

As Congress states, "The special operations forces of the Armed Forces provide the United States with immediate and primary capability to respond to terrorism." Moreover, in the view of Congress, Special Operations Forces are "the military mainstay of the United States for the purpose of nation-building and training friendly foreign forces in order to preclude deployment or combat involving the conventional or strategic forces of the United States."[1]

Statutory Responsibilities

Congress identifies in the following order 10 activities that focus SOF efforts "insofar as [each] relates to special operations:"[2]

- Direct Action (DA)
- Strategic Reconnaissance (SR)
- Unconventional Warfare (UW)
- Foreign Internal Defense (FID)
- Civil Affairs (CA)
- Psychological Operations (PSYOP)
- Counterterrorism (CT)
- Humanitarian Assistance (HA)
- Theater Search and Rescue (TSAR)
- Such other activities as may be specified by the President or the Secretary of Defense

The Secretary of Defense and Commander in Chief, United States Special Operations Command (CINCSOC) consider the first six entries to be primary responsibilities. Humanitarian assistance and TSAR occupy a separate category called "collateral special operations activities," together with such disparate duties as antiterrorism (the defensive counterpart of counterterrorism), counterdrug operations, and security assistance.[3]

Direct Action

Direct actions are short-duration, small-scale offensive activities such as raids, ambushes, hostage rescues, and "surgical" strikes to neutralize, seize, or destroy critical targets that could include weapons of mass destruction and associated production facilities. SOF excel at such operations and in many cases possess applicable skills that conventional forces cannot duplicate.[4]

Strategic (Special) Reconnaissance

SR operations, which DoD doctrine redesignates as "special" reconnaisance, collect or verify three sorts of information of national or theater-level significance: 1) the capabilities, intentions, and activities of actual and potential enemies; 2) geographic, demographic, and other regional characteristics; and 3) post-strike battle damage assessments. Land, sea, and air SOF conduct clandestine operations that other forces seldom can duplicate in hostile or denied territory under politically sensitive conditions.

Unconventional Warfare

U.S. unconventional warfare activities primarily assist insurgents, secessionists, and resistance movements abroad. Special Operations Forces assigned such missions help organize, equip, train, and advise indigenous undergrounds and guerrillas, furnish various kinds of support, and establish evasion/escape networks that facilitate safe movement to, from, and within enemy territory.

Foreign Internal Defense

FID involves U.S. interdepartmental/interagency efforts to help a foreign government forestall or defeat insurgency, lawlessness, or subversion. Operations seek to strengthen host nation political, economic, social, and national security institutions. SOF primarily train, advise, and otherwise assist local military and paramilitary forces that perform such functions.

Civil Affairs

CA activities promote civil-military cooperation between U.S. military forces and foreign governments, foreign populations, and nongovernmental organizations at national and local levels before, during, and after hostilities or other emergencies. They may also administer occupied areas and assist friendly governments in rebuilding civil infrastructure and institutions. CA forces support special as well as conventional operations.

Psychological Operations

PSYOP activities involve the planned use of propaganda and actions to influence the opinions, emotions, attitudes, and behavior of friends, neutrals, and enemies in ways that assist accomplishment of security objectives before, during, and after hostilities. PSYOP forces support special as well as conventional operations.

Counterterrorism

CT concerns offensive interdepartmental/interagency measures designed to deter and, if necessary, defeat domestic and transnational terrorism. Special Mission Units designed expressly for these purposes are prepared to preempt or resolve terrorist incidents primarily abroad, but may advise, train, and indirectly assist other CT forces of the U.S. Government inside the United States if directed to do so by the President or Secretary of Defense.

Humanitarian Assistance

Humanitarian assistance primarily attempts to improve the quality of life in foreign countries. *Title 10* limits DoD activities to the following: medical, dental, and veterinary care in rural areas; rudimentary surface transportation, well drilling, and basic sanitation projects; rudimentary construction and repair of public facilities; and transportation of relief supplies. DoD interprets humanitarian assistance more broadly. Disaster relief operations in the United States also occur occasionally.

Theater Search and Rescue

TSAR activities involve the use of aircraft, surface craft, submarines, specialized teams, and equipment to find and recover pilots and aircrews downed on land or at sea outside the United States and its territorial waters. Combat search and rescue operations often require special skills and equipment that enable small teams to infiltrate enemy territory undetected, accomplish their missions, and return clandestinely.

Contrast with Conventional Forces

Counterterrorism and unconventional warfare are strictly special operations. SOF share the other seven specific responsibilities with conventional forces, but because low-visibility low-cost special operations techniques are distinctively different, they expand the range of options open to U.S. defense decisionmakers.

Special operations often are employable where high-profile conventional forces appear to be politically, militarily, or economically inappropriate. Small, self-reliant, readily deployable units that capitalize on speed, surprise, audacity, and deception may sometimes accomplish missions in ways that minimize risks of escalation and concurrently maximize returns compared with orthodox applications of military power, which normally emphasize mass. Aircraft, artillery, or combat engineers, for example, might demolish a critical bridge at a particular time, but SOF could magnify the physical and psychological effects considerably if they blew that bridge while a trainload of enemy dignitaries or ammunition was halfway across. Conventional land, sea, and air forces normally patrol specified sectors intermittently, whereas special reconnaissance troops may remain in hostile territory for weeks or months at a time collecting information that otherwise would be unobtainable.[5] Severe misfortunes, of course, may accompany failure. Large enemy conventional forces can easily overwhelm small SOF units they manage to corner during clandestine operations and may be tempted to treat survivors harshly. Adverse political repercussions can be far reaching.

"Nontraditional" responsibilities, such as humanitarian assistance, are traditional roles for Army Special Forces, PSYOP, and Civil Affairs units. Their readiness, in fact, *improves* while they perform foreign internal defense missions, whereas the combat readiness of conventional forces normally *declines*, because such duties divert time and attention from primary responsibilities. Area orientation and language skills attune these SOF (and some SEALs) to cultural nuances that usually temper humanitarian assistance techniques. Self-reliance allows them to function effectively under austere conditions without the infrastructure that conventional forces often need.[6]

Notes

1. Section 1453, *Department of Defense Authorization Act, 1986*, (P.L. 99-145; 99 Stat. 760), 29 July 1985.

2. Section 167 (j), *Title 10, United States Code (Armed Forces)*.

3. Secretary of Defense, *Annual Report to the President and Congress* (Washington, DC: GPO, 1993), 106; James R. Locher III and General Carl W. Stiner, *United States Special Operations Forces: Posture Statement* (Washington, DC: Assistant Secretary of Defense (SO/LIC), 1992), 3-4.

4. For greater detail concerning all SOF missions, see *Joint Pub 3-05: Doctrine for Joint Special Operations* (Washington, DC: Office of the Chairman, Joint Chiefs of Staff, 1992), II 2-15. See also "Special Operations Issues," a critique in John M. Collins, *Roles and Functions of U.S. Combat Forces*, Rpt. 93-72S (Washington, DC: Congressional Research Service, 1993), 45-60.

5. *Congressional Research Service (CRS) Study on SOF: Responses to Questions*, ASD SO/LIC memorandum, 25 June 1993, 1-2.

6. Ibid., p. 3-4; Lieutenant Colonel Bernard V. Moore II, *U.S. Special Operations Forces: Their Unique Value to the Nation's Security* (Washington, DC: Hq USAF (XOXS), 1993); *Characteristics of Special Operations: SOF vs. Conventional*, briefing slides, Fort Bragg, NC, Joint Special Operations Command, April 1993; Laurence Jolidon, "Aspin Picking 'Pockets': Military Says Relief Efforts Hurt Readiness," *USA Today*, 27 April 1993, 4.

II. Initial Problems, Initiatives, and Compliance

To appreciate SOF progress, persistent deficiencies, and future courses of action, it is necessary to review Congressional legislation related to special operations in the late 1980s: Congress enacted Public Law (P.L.) 99-661 in 1986, and P.L. 100-180 and P.L. 100-456 soon followed, because initial implementation seemed unsatisfactory. Until recently, results of these actions received mixed reviews in the special operations community as well as on Capitol Hill.[1]

Perceived Problems

U.S. Special Operations Forces crested during the 1960s when they played prominent roles in Vietnam, Laos, and Cambodia. They wallowed in a trough after U.S. armed forces withdrew from Southeast Asia. Nine active Army Special Forces group equivalents shrank to three, and one was scheduled for deactivation. SOF aircraft suffered similar cuts or reverted to reserve, and the Navy decommissioned its only special operations submarine. SOF manning levels in every service dropped well below authorized strengths. Funding declined precipitously, to about one-tenth of 1 percent of the U.S. defense budget by 1975. SOF planning and programming expertise eroded rapidly.[2]

Congressional Actions

The failed rescue of hostages held in Teheran provided a wake-up call in April 1980.[3] A few modest improvements followed that failure, but strong resistance to change persisted. Service decisionmakers consistently siphoned off special operations funds for conventional forces, and frustration mounted in both Armed Services Committees until Congress took action.[4]

Public Law 99-661, 1986

Section 1311 of P.L. 99-661, commonly called the Cohen-Nunn Amendment, mandated the creation of a United States Special Operations Command (USSOCOM). The President, through the Secretary of Defense with advice and assistance from the Joint Chiefs of Staff, had previously established and prescribed force structures for all unified combatant commands in accord with Section 161, *Title 10, United States Code*. Section 1311, which became law on 14 November 1986 despite vigorous Pentagon objections, called for five organizational and budgetary innovations:

- *A Board for Low-Intensity Conflict within the National Security Council (NSC)*. It was the sense of Congress that the President should designate a Deputy Assistant to the President for National Security Affairs who would serve as the Deputy Assistant for Low-Intensity Conflict.

- *An Assistant Secretary of Defense for Special Operations and Low-Intensity Conflict (ASD SO/LIC)*. The principal intended duty was overall supervision of special operations activities, including oversight of policy and resources.

- *A unified combatant command for special operations forces*. All active and reserve SOF in the United States were to be assigned. The Commander in Chief of U.S. Special Operations Command (CINCSOC) was to develop strategy, doctrine, and tactics; train assigned forces; conduct specialized courses of instruction for commissioned and noncommissioned officers; validate requirements; establish priorities; ensure combat readiness; prepare budget requests for special operations-peculiar weapons, equipment, supplies, and services; and otherwise promote SOF professionalism. Additionally, CINCSOC was responsible for monitoring the preparedness of special operations forces assigned to other unified combatant commands.

■ *A Major Force Program (MFP)-11.* The Secretary of Defense was to create a new budgetary category that would integrate SOF requirements into DoD's Five-Year Defense Plan. The ASD SO/LIC would oversee the preparation and submission of program recommendations and budget proposals by CINCSOC. Only the Secretary of Defense could revise SOF programs and budgets approved by Congress, after consulting with CINCSOC.

■ *The SOF commander in U.S. European Command, U.S. Pacific Command, and any other U.S. unified combatant command designated by the Secretary of Defense to be of general or flag rank.* This stipulation was designed to strengthen the influence and effectiveness of Special Operations Forces around the world.

Public Law 100-180, 1987

Congress enacted Section 1211, P.L. 100-180 on 4 December 1987, because conferees felt "forced by bureaucratic resistance within the Department of Defense to take very detailed legislative action in mandating the urgently needed reorganization and reform of special operations and low-intensity conflict capabilities, policies and programs."[5] Mandates included the following actions:

■ *The ASD SO/LIC became the principal civilian adviser to the Secretary of Defense on special operations and low-intensity conflict matters.* The first incumbent was to "report directly, without intervening review or approval, to the Secretary of Defense personally or, as designated by the Secretary, to the Deputy Secretary of Defense personally.

■ *The Secretary of Defense was directed to publish a charter for the ASD SO/LIC.* Its contents were to include duties, responsibilities, authority, relationships with other DoD officials, and miscellaneous matters.

■ *The Secretary of the Army was designated as acting ASD SO/LIC until the office was formally filled for the first time.* He was to submit monthly progress reports to the Senate and House Armed Services Committees.

- *CINCSOC acquired Head of Agency authority to facilitate the development and procurement of special operations peculiar hardware.* CINCSOC's staff was to include an inspector general who would conduct internal audits, inspect contracting/purchasing arrangements, and otherwise facilitate the implementation of MFP-11, which was to be created not later than 30 days after P.L. 100-180 was enacted.

Public Law 100-456, 1988

SOF programming and budgeting problems persisted, despite passage of the two previous laws in 1986 and 1987. Congress therefore enacted clarifying legislation on 29 September 1988. P.L. 100-456 provided that:

- *CINCSOC should prepare and submit to the Secretary of Defense SOF program recommendations and budget proposals.* This would allow authority, direction, and control over the expenditure of funds for all forces under his command.

- *Congress extended those powers to include SOF assigned to unified commands other than USSOCOM.*

Compliance in the 1980s

Implementation of these three laws proceeded slowly despite constant pressure from concerned Members of Congress, who repeatedly expressed their displeasure to the Secretary of Defense. Misunderstanding and deep-seated distrust were apparent, because accomplishments generally reflected compliance with the letter rather than the spirit of each law.[6] President Ronald Reagan's 1987 *Report to the Congress on U.S. Capabilities to Engage in Low-Intensity Conflict and Conduct Special Operations* generated caustic critiques during congressional hearings,[7] and as late as 1989, Congress still perceived a long list of uncorrected defects.

Accomplishments by 1989

An NSC Board for Low-Intensity Conflict, chaired by the President's Special Assistant for National Security Affairs, began operations in October 1987, and working groups thereafter met at least monthly.[8]

The Senate confirmed the first Assistant Secretary of Defense (SO/LIC) in July 1988, 14 months beyond the date P.L. 99-661 prescribed, and confirmed the first Commander in Chief of USSOCOM in April 1987. Combatant command of all active and most reserve component Special Operations Forces, including SEALs (which the Navy had hoped to hold), passed to USSOCOM shortly thereafter.[9]

Shortcomings in 1989

Some achievements lose luster when put in perspective. The Low-Intensity Conflict Board in the NSC held no plenary sessions until 1990, and even then its influence was slight. The ASD SO/LIC lost direct access to the Secretary of Defense in August 1989 after Charles Whitehouse, the first incumbent, left office.[10] James R. Locher III, his successor, shared important responsibilities with other Pentagon officials—psychological operations, civil affairs, humanitarian assistance, and certain classified compartmentalized intelligence activities among others.[11] CINCSOC and his staff could develop doctrine and tactics in the absence of sound policy guidance from the National Security Council and ASD SO/LIC, but special operations strategies that prioritize particular roles, functions, and missions in particular regions around the world remained out of reach.[12]

Notes

1. For two overviews, see Colonel William G. Boykin, *Special Operations and Low-Intensity Conflict Legislation: Why It Was Passed and Have the Voids Been Filled?*, Military Studies Program Paper (Carlisle Barracks, PA: U.S. Army War College, 1991); Jim Nichol, *Special Operations and Low-Intensity Conflict: U.S. Progress and Problems*, Issue Brief IB 90091 (Washington, DC: Congressional Research Service, 1990, archived).

2. Boykin, 5-6; Congress, House, Noel C. Koch, *Statement Before the Special Operations Panel*, Subcommittee on Readiness, HASC, 6 September 1984, 2; Jim Wootten, *Special Operations Forces: Issues for Congress*, 84-227 F (Washington, DC: Congressional Research Service, 1984), 1-4.

3. *Rescue Mission Report* (the Holloway Report) (Washington, DC: Joint Chiefs of Staff Special Operations Review Group, 1980); Colonel Charlie Beckwith and Donald Knox, *Delta Force* (NY: Harcourt Brace

Jovanovich, 1983), 187-300.

4.   Congressman Dan Daniel, "The Case for a Sixth Service," *Armed Forces Journal*, August 1985, p. 70, 72, 74-75; Boykin, 10-33.

5.   Congress, House, *National Defense Authorization Act for Fiscal Years 1988 and 1989*, Conference Report to Accompany H.R. 1748 (Report 100-446), 100th Cong., 1st sess., 17 November 1987, 682.

6.   Boykin, 38-56; Nichol, 5-15.

7.   Congress, House, *Special Operations Forces*, Hearings before the Special Operations Panel and the Readiness Subcommittee of the Committee on Armed Services, H.A.S.C. No. 100-58, 100th Cong., 2d sess.

8.   Congress, House, *Special Operations Forces,* 16-17.

9.   Memorandum for the Secretary of Defense through the Under Secretary of Defense for Policy from the Assistant Secretary of Defense (International Security Affairs), *Assignment of Naval Special Warfare (NSW) Groups to USSOCOM*, 9 October 1987; memoranda from Secretary of Defense Weinberger to Chairman of the Joint Chiefs of Staff and the Secretary of the Navy, *Assignment of Naval Special Warfare (NSW) Groups to CINCSOC*, 23 October 1987.

10. Rules and Regulations, , 32 CFR Part 385, "Under Secretary of Defense for Policy," *Federal Register* (15 August 1989), vol. 54, no. 156, 33521-23.

11. Boykin, 53-54; Nichol, 8.

12. Boykin, 48; for some policy considerations, see Congress, House, *Special Operations Forces*, 36-37.

III. High Command and Control Arrangements

The performance of SOF roles and missions depends in large part on the proficiency of high command figures who pick subordinates; establish policies; develop strategies, doctrines, and tactics; set standards for and supervise training; plan, program, and budget; integrate activities; conduct operations; and otherwise seek to ensure that the whole possesses capabilities greater than the sum of its parts.

The National Security Council, the Assistant Secretary of Defense (SO/LIC), the Commander in Chief of U.S. Special Operations Command, other unified combatant commanders, Congress, and associated staffs all are key players (figure 1). Although overall performance has improved substantially since 1989, the record of achievement is uneven.

NSC Guidance and Oversight

Other than the Department of Defense, the National Security Council (NSC) is the only U.S. organization theoretically able to develop overarching guidance and to supervise implementation that involves many arms of the U.S. Government, including the Departments of State; Justice (Federal Bureau of Investigation, Border Patrol, U.S. Marshals Service); Transportation (Coast Guard, Federal Aviation Administration); Energy; Treasury (Customs Service; Bureau of Alcohol, Tobacco and Firearms); the Central Intelligence Agency; U.S. Information Agency; and the Drug Enforcement Administration. No other organization is as well positioned as the NSC to institutionalize team play at the top.

Figure 1. *Special Operations High Command*

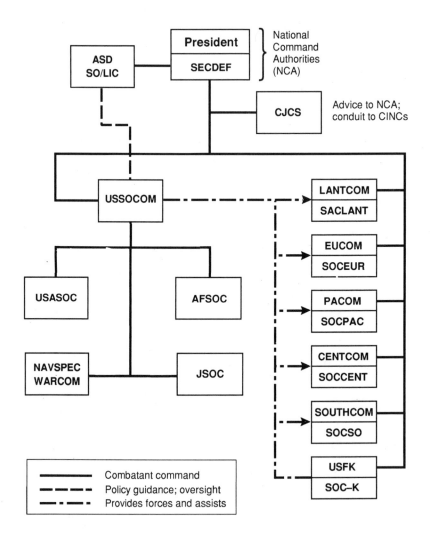

Note: See appendix D for abbreviations

The Board for Low-Intensity Conflict (LIC), activated to serve some (but not all) of these purposes, looked impressive on paper during the Bush Administration. The Assistant to the President for National Security Affairs, who also was Senior Director for International Programs and held ambassadorial rank, chaired the Deputies Committee in its capacity as the LIC Board, on which second-rank officials from all pertinent departments and agencies were represented.[1] The only full-time board member was the *de facto* staff director. The only major project was an "interagency review of how the U.S. Government formulates, coordinates, resources, and implements national security strategy and policy related to lesser developed countries threatened by or engaged in a low-intensity conflict, specifically insurgency."[2] The Board interviewed "active Executive branch officials from all relevant departments and agencies, former government officials, members of Congress, and others from the private and public sectors who have an interest in and knowledge of LIC".[3] Ten rather bland recommendations ensued in May 1991, after 18 months. One proposed a Policy Coordinating Committee for Low-Intensity Conflict. The Department of State disapproved, whereupon the entire project died. No further efforts followed.[4] The Clinton Administration has not established a Board for Low-Intensity Conflict, nor has it announced intentions to do so.

OSD Guidance and Oversight

The ASD SO/LIC "is the Principal Staff Assistant and civilian adviser to the Secretary of Defense for policy and planning related to SO/LIC activities within the Department of Defense."[5] He is one of 11 Assistant Secretaries of Defense, but is unlike any of his nominal peers:

- Responsibilities resemble those of service secretaries in some respects, because they include "the overall preparation and justification of program recommendations and budget proposals for [special operations] activities in the Five Year Defense Plan." The ASD SO/LIC further advises the Under Secretary of Defense (Acquisition) on "priorities and requirements for SO-and LIC-related material and equipment" and, together with CINCSOC, presents SO and LIC programs to Congress.[6]

- In other respects, the Assistant Secretary of Defense for Special Operations and Low-Intensity Conflict shares responsibilities with the Chairman of the Joint Chiefs of Staff (CJCS), because the SO/LIC charter tells the ASD to "translate national security policy objectives into specific defense policy objectives achievable by designated SO and LIC activities ... conduct studies and analyses ... oversee an integrated development and refinement of doctrines, strategies, and processes for SO and LIC; prepare overall plans and implementation guidance for the various areas in the world where SO and LIC objectives exist," oversee readiness, assess strengths and weaknesses, and "recommend to the Secretary of Defense legislative initiatives to enhance SO and LIC capabilities."

Neither Charles Whitehouse, who was ASD SO/LIC from August 1988 to June 1989, nor James R. Locher III, his successor until June 1993, were special operations practitioners before appointment; therefore on-the-job training was essential.

Locher had other impediments to overcome. Pentagon occupants initially viewed him as a "fox in the chicken coop," because he had helped craft opposed SO/LIC legislation. Loosely defined limits of low-intensity conflict, which officially comprises "a full range of offensive and defensive measures,"[7] still encourage competition between the ASD SO/LIC and five military services (Army, Navy, Air Force, Marine Corps, and Coast Guard), which furnish conventional forces for LIC purposes and fight for related funds. Locher originally lacked clear authority to oversee psychological operations, civil affairs, and humanitarian assistance, although all three are special operations activities according to *Title 10, United States Code*.[8] Conflicts with the JCS Chairman, the Joint Staff, and USSOCOM over planning responsibilities remain unresolved.

Successive Secretaries of Defense have declined to correct such conditions. They also have denied ASD SO/LIC requests for additional staff to deal with counternarcotics and compartmentalized special operations intelligence (the ASD for Reserve Affairs was DoD's Drug Enforcement Coordinator during the Bush Administration; the ASD for Command, Control, Communications, and Intelligence handled SO intelligence). A draft DoD Directive indicates that the Under Secretary of Defense for Policy will assume those and other SO/LIC responsibilities during the

Clinton Administration.[9]

Functions of USSOCOM

The U.S. Special Operations Command is unlike any other regionally oriented U.S. unified combatant command in several significant respects:[10]

- USSOCOM is a unified command, but receives guidance from the ASD SO/LIC and the ASD for Program Analysis and Evaluation as well as from the Secretary of Defense through the Chairman of the Joint Chiefs of Staff. CINCSOC, unlike regionally oriented unified commanders, has no Area of Responsibility (AOR) and commands "selected special operations" only on rare occasions when the President or Secretary of Defense so direct. CINCSOC must negotiate Command Arrangements Agreements (CAA) with each Theater Commander Chief.[11]

- USSOCOM somewhat resembles a military service because it prepares forces for use by regionally oriented combatant commands. CINCSOC thereafter merely monitors activities of SOF employed in each theater. Like each service chief, the CINCSOC has R&D responsibilities and presents program/budget proposals peculiar to the command. USSOCOM, however, does not recruit personnel. Assigned officers as well as rank and file depend on their parent services for assignments and promotion. CINCSOC merely monitors. USSOCOM moreover must negotiate separate Memoranda of Agreement (MOA) with the Army, Navy and Air Force, which furnish all support that is not considered SOF-specific.[12]

- USSOCOM also exercises Head of Agency authority and receives funds for such purposes. Its programming, budgeting, research, and development responsibilities cut across Service lines. The Under Secretary of Defense for Acquisition oversees related activities. Defense agencies, however, typically advise, assist, and support the entire U.S. defense community. The U.S. Special Operations Command does not.[13]

Competition for assignment as CINCSOC thus far has been confined to a very small group, because few senior officers who climbed the promotion ladder to three or four stars accumulated much special operations experience en route. This group includes Lieutenant General Samuel V. Wilson, who logged more than 11 years of SOF experience at every level from lieutenant to colonel, and General Robert C. Kingston, who had six diversified tours that totalled 10 years at every level from lieutenant to brigadier general, including unconventional warfare combat in Korea and Southeast Asia. Both retired before 1987. Only seven potential candidates for CINCSOC in 1987 had any special operations qualifications. The first selectee, General James J. Lindsay, had briefly commanded a Special Forces "A" Team as a captain. Initially, therefore, on-the-job training was obligatory. General Carl W. Stiner, Lindsay's successor, logged considerably more time with SOF before he became CINC, having first served as a captain with the 3rd Special Forces Group, then commanding the Joint Special Operations Command (JSOC) as a major general from 1984 to 1986, for a total of almost 6 years.[14] General Wayne A. Downing, the current CINCSOC, had six SOF assignments after he was promoted to lieutenant colonel. Fortunately, the pool of generals and admirals with extensive special operations experience is gradually growing.

Selected officers and enlisted personnel from the recently deactivated U.S. Readiness Command comprised most of the USSOCOM staff from 1987 to 1988. Fewer than 20 percent were experienced Special Operations Forces. SOF currently assigned fall somewhat short of General Lindsay's goal, which was to triple that percentage. By mid-1993 the roster reflected about 30 percent: 116 out of 397, including 35 Army Special Forces, 27 Rangers, 17 SEALs, and 35 Air Force SOF (not all "Rangers" noted served with the Ranger Regiment; some simply graduated from a Ranger training course).[15] The USSOCOM staff also includes PSYOP and civil affairs officers, who occupy categories that the Secretary of Defense designated as SOF on 2 March 1993.[16]

Relations between USSOCOM and regionally oriented U.S. combatant commands that employ most SOF generally are good, but this was not always so. Squabbles over control occurred, for example, when Special Mission Units deployed. Their first chief confided that "two separate Unified Commanders once told me that they understood my charter from the [Chairman of the Joint Chiefs of Staff and the Secretary of Defense], but when I or my Special Operations Forces step foot in their area of responsibility that all changes. The moment the CINC learns that you have direct communications with your headquarters and to the CJCS he becomes hostile. In every instance the CINC insisted those nets not be open."[17]

Interactions between USSOCOM and other unified commands subsequently improved, according to General Stiner, who believes the current crop of CINCs understand and appreciate SOF much better than most of their predecessors.[18]

Theater Special Operations Commands

U.S. Atlantic Command (LANTCOM), European Command (EUCOM), Pacific Command (PACOM), Central Command (CENTCOM), and Southern Command (SOUTHCOM) each contain a theater special operations command (SOC) that is a subordinate unified command with a broad, continuing mission. Special Operations Command, Korea (SOC-K), a small standing joint task force, supports U.S. Forces Korea. Each SOC plans for, commands, controls, exercises, and otherwise prepares SOF that USSOCOM organizes, equips, trains, tailors, and provides to regional CINCs whose distinctive requirements reflect different political, military, cultural, and geographic environments. Each SOC additionally seeks to ensure that its commander-in-chief, staff, and component commands understand the utility of SOF and how to synchronize their activities with conventional military operations.[19]

Congress originally decreed that SOC commanders in EUCOM and PACOM "shall be of general or flag officer grade," but allowed the Secretary of Defense to designate others if he saw fit. Officers in charge of special operations commands in CENTCOM and SOUTHCOM subsequently have been authorized one star, in conformance with congressional recommendations in July 1992. The increasing importance of SOF "as the United States shifts its security forces to regional and low intensity conflicts" furnished the rationale.[20]

CINCSOC exercises authority, direction, and control over the expenditure of funds for SOF assigned to regionally oriented unified combatant commands with respect to the development and acquisition of special operations-peculiar equipment and the acquisition of special operations-peculiar material, supplies, and services. Similar powers over other SOC funds may be exercised "to the extent directed by the Secretary of Defense."[21] Those prescriptions have worked fairly well, despite the potential for conflicts of interest between CINCSOC and the supported theater commanders. Modifications to existing Command Arrangements Agreements should smooth out present relationships.[22]

Congressional Oversight

Special operations have never had a large constituency in Congress, but the few Members and staff who expressed concern in the mid-1980s exerted great influence that culminated in SO/LIC legislation already discussed.[23] Senators Nunn and Cohen, who were prominent among them, still champion SOF. Unfortunately, Congressman Dan Daniel, a strong SOF proponent on the House Armed Services Committee, has died, and several able and persuasive staffers have been reassigned.   Hearings to ascertain compliance with laws, progress, and persistent limitations ceased after 1988, when the House Armed Services Committee disbanded its Special Operations Panel.

Congressional interests nevertheless continue. Members and staff stay abreast of developments through personal contact with key officials in the special operations community and trips to observe activities.   Both Armed Services and Appropriations Committees review SOF programs, annual budget requests, and otherwise oversee special operations.

Notes

1.   Telephone conversation with Colonel Christopher J. Needels, NSC Director of International Programs and *de facto* staff director of the Board for Low-Intensity Conflict during the Bush Administration, 12 April 1993.

2.   Invitational letter from Ambassador David C. Miller, Jr., Special Assistant to the President for National Security Affairs, 21 May 1990.

3.   *National Security Review of Low-Intensity Conflict* (Washington,DC: National Security Council, May 1991); Needels, 1993.

4.   Telephone conversation with NSC officials, 14 April 1993.

5.   *Department of Defense Directive 5138.3*, "Assistant Secretary of Defense (Special Operations and Low Intensity Conflict)," 4 January 1988.

6. For responsibilities of Service Secretaries, see *Title 10, United States Code*, Sections 3013-3014, 5013-5014, 8013-8014.

7. Ibid, 1-2; Congress, House, *Special Operations Forces*, Hearings Before the Special Operations Panel and the Readiness Subcommittee of the Committee on Armed Services, H.A.S.C. No. 100-58, 100th Cong., 2d sess., 1988, 26-27, 33-34, 54-55.

8. Colonel William G. Boykin, *Special Operations and Low-Intensity Conflict Legislation*, Military Studies Program Paper (Carlisle Barracks, PA: U.S. Army War College, 1991), 53-54; Jim Nichol, *Special Operations and Low-Intensity Conflict*, Issue Brief IB 90091 (Washington, DC: Congressional Research Service, 1990, Archived), 8.

9. Tony Capaccio, "Cheney Rebuffs Bid to Boost Special Ops Staff," *Defense Week*, 12 March 1990, 1, 5; "Reporter's Notebook," *Defense Week*, 19 March 1990, 4.; *Draft Department of Defense Directive: Under Secretary of Defense for Policy (USD (P))*, undated.

10. Jill M. Blickstein and Steven C. Grundman, *Implementing Special Operations Reforms*, report prepared for the Principal Deputy Assistant Secretary of Defense for Program Analysis and Evaluation (Cambridge, MA: John F. Kennedy School of Government, Harvard University, 1989), 18-20.

11. For responsibilities of U.S. combatant commands, see *Title 10, United States Code*, chapter 6.

12. For common functions of U.S. military services, see *Department of Defense Directive 5100.1*, "Functions of the Department of Defense and Its Major Components," 25 September 1987, 10-13. See also *Special Operations Command: Progress Made In Completing Needed Agreements*, Report Nr. GAO/NSIAD-92-109 (Washington, DC: General Accounting Office, 1992).

13. Relationships between defense agencies and other DoD components are described in the *Federal Register* (19 January 1989), vol. 54, vo. 12, 2101-2111.

14. Biographic summaries of Generals Downing, Kingston, Lindsay, Stiner, and Wilson; correspondence from Secretary of Defense Caspar Weinberger to Congressman Earl Hutto, Chairman of the Special Operations Panel, House Armed Services Committee, 16 April 1987.

15. Telephone conversation with General James J. Lindsay, 3 March 1988; data derived from USSOCOM, 20 April 1993.

16. *Designation of Psychological Operations and Civil Affairs as Special Operations Forces*, memorandum from the Secretary of Defense to Secretaries of the Military Departments and Chairman of the Joint Chiefs of Staff, 3 March 1993.

17. Major General Richard A. Scholtes, *Some Thoughts on Forming a Very Special Organization*, a presentation to members of Betac Corporation, 16 January 1987, 4-5. A summary of Scholtes' testimony before Congress in August 1986 on a related subject is contained in Boykin, 28-29.

18. Comments by General Carl W. Stiner at Fort Bragg, NC, 30 March 1993, amplified in a telephone conversation on 19 April 1993.

19. James R. Locher III and General Carl W. Stiner, *United States Special Operations Forces: Posture Statement* (Washington, DC: Assistant Secretary of Defense [SO/LIC], 1993), B 5-9.

20. Section 1311, P.L. 99-661, 14 November 1986; Congress, Senate, Committee on Armed Services, *National Defense Authorization Act for Fiscal Year 1993*, Report 102-352, to accompany S. 3114, 102d Cong., 2d sess., 1992, 277.

21. Section 167 (e) (2) (C) and (e) (4) (A), *Title 10, United States Code.*

22. Telephone conversation with Margaret Kinkead in USSOCOM Washington Office, 10 May 1993.

23. Boykin, 10-38.

IV. Progress by ASD SO/LIC and USSOCOM

The Office of the Assistant Secretary of Defense for Special Operations and Low-Intensity Conflict (ASD SO/LIC) and the U.S. Special Operations Command have made impressive strides since 1987. Professional staff work, intensive training, and diversified practical experience have reshaped and strengthened SOF. Progress has been uneven, but significant improvements are evident.

ASD SO/LIC Accomplishments

The ASD SO/LIC has accomplished quite a lot with a relatively small staff since Congress confirmed the first occupant of that office in August 1988. A Principal Deputy is second in command; one Deputy Assistant ASD handles policy and missions, another covers forces and resources. Authorized personnel strength is 77 (42 military, 35 civilians), including administrative support. Civilians are preponderant in supervisory positions, but several of them accrued 20 years or more of SOF experience while in the Army, Navy, or Air Force. "Action officers" with extensive military service (not necessarily SOF) outnumber career civil servants by about five-to-one; proven interdepartmental and interagency performers who know how to work within the system are among them.[1]

Few ASD SO/LIC achievements have been well publicized. Most occurred quietly and incrementally, but the cumulative influence on institutional relationships, policies, and plans has been considerable.

Influence on Defense Organization

Organizational initiatives by ASD SO/LIC have sought to clarify relationships with USSOCOM and strengthen intelligence support. The most conspicuous successes, however, center on civil affairs, psychological operations, and anti/counterterrorism, as indicated in this summary of accomplishments:[2]

- Strengthened and clarified organizational relationships between ASD SO/LIC and USSOCOM by developing 10 mutually agreeable principles to improve coordination and oversight and by resolving legal disagreements over defining elements of ASD SO/LIC oversight and supervision of USSOCOM activities.

- Directed an independent evaluation of USSOCOM headquarters manpower requirements. This evaluation validated additional personnel spaces needed to perform the necessary headquarters functions to support SOF.

- Promulgated a DoD/CIA Memorandum of Agreement (MOA) in coordination with other offices within OSD and the Joint Staff that articulates CIA support for military operations. This effort updated three outmoded MOAs between DoD/CIA.

- Successfully represented continuing needs for the Sensitive Special Operations Program on matters dealing with operational and policy decisions during the DoD intelligence reorganization. ASD SO/LIC's relationship with the intelligence community has proven to be a key ingredient for negotiating sensitive intelligence support for the special operations community.

- Persuaded the Secretary of Defense in March 1993 to designate civil affairs and psychological operations forces as Special Operations Forces. That decision helped to eliminate the fragmentation of civil affairs responsibilities among other OSD offices.

- Formed a DoD Civil Affairs Working Group composed of representatives from OSD, the Joint Staff, the services, and USSOCOM. The Working Group serves as a centralized forum for discussing and coordinating civil affairs policies and activities.

- Established a DoD International Information Committee to enhance interaction and coordination among psychological operations staff officers of OSD, Joint Staff, and the services.

- Instituted procedures to substantially reduce interagency approval times for PSYOP programs. Theater CINCs once had to wait months for approval.

- Persuaded the Secretary of Defense in 1988 to designate ASD SO/LIC as the single point of contact for DoD antiterrorism matters, thereby linking efforts of the Joint Staff, unified and specified commands, defense agencies, and the interagency antiterrorism community.

- Represented OSD in the interagency community for combatting terrorism. Developed the DoD *Long-range Combatting Terrorism Policy Master Plan*, which includes assessments of current policies, programs, and potential terrorist threats in the years 2000, 2010, and 2025 and strategies to combat future terrorism. As the DoD single point of contact for antiterrorism matters (defensive measures against terrorism), ASD SO/LIC worked closely with the military services to improve the security of U.S. military forces stationed overseas.

Influence On Policies and Plans

Initiatives by the ASD SO/LIC have encouraged the Secretary of Defense and his principal assistants to integrate SOF more fully and effectively into policies and plans, according to the ASD's accomplishment summary:[3]

- Developed and promulgated policy directives regarding the planning, programming, budgeting, execution, and acquisition authority granted to USSOCOM.

- Justified enhanced funding for SOF research, development, and acquisition programs. Efforts will contribute to improved future capabilities.

- Co-directed with the Joint Staff an initiative to identify requirements for operations short of war based on inputs from unified and specified commanders. This process verified that military peacetime operations and responses to low-intensity conflict situations are at the core of CINC theater strategies and require commensurate guidance and resources.

- Completed two comprehensive policy documents that provide unprecedented general guidance on Special Operations Forces and operations short of war and contribute to such critical national security documents as the Defense Planning Guidance (DPG) and the National Military Strategy. In the case of the DPG, obtained an order of magnitude increase in attention to SOF force structure and missions.

- Developed extensive input for the *Bottom-Up Review*, a zero-based examination of roles for U.S. Armed Forces in the emerging security environment. The project, aimed at improving SOF effectiveness in accomplishing traditional and new missions, included policy proposals for strategic forward basing of SOF; afloat bases for SOF in regions where land-based presence is not feasible; research, development, and acquisition initiatives to improve SOF contribution to counterproliferation; a range of activities to improve national assistance capabilities; and recommendations concerning such missions as peacekeeping, peacemaking, promoting democracy, and nonproliferation.

- Buttressed the national campaign to counter the proliferation of weapons of mass destruction by ensuring that current SOF capabilities are being integrated into key strategy documents and policy decisions and by sponsoring multiyear, multi-agency research studies that explore emerging and potential counterproliferation roles for SOF.

- Authored U.S. counterterrorism (offensive measures) policy in response to major contingencies and international incidents, such as the Olympic Games, Pan Am 103, and Somalia.

- Evaluated security for the 1992 Olympics. An ASD SO/LIC representative led the U.S. Interagency Waterside Security Working Group which evaluated coastal security in Barcelona before the Olympics and recommended equipment and training to strengthen countermeasures.

- Proposed and oversaw implementation of two legislative changes and one DoD directive that enhance overseas training opportunities for SOF; establish DoD policy for SOF foreign language capabilities; and provide a mechanism for modernizing the military forces in drug-producing countries through the transfer of excess defense articles. The SOF training legislation included civil affairs and psychological operations forces previously not covered in legislative authorities, deleted requirements that CINCs ensure mutual training benefits for both U.S. and host-nation forces, and allowed funding for the training of SOF with friendly foreign forces.

- Undertook 38 research projects to resolve key policy and resource issues. The spectrum covers such diversified subjects as information management, technical intelligence, peacetime engagement, weapon proliferation, and prerequisites for successful special operations.[4]

Influence on Perceptions of SOF

Efforts to correct misimpressions of SOF and apprise conventional commanders/staffs of SOF missions, capabilities, and limitations are immensely important. The ASD SO/LIC has been a steadfast contributor. Prime accomplishments include:[5]

- Publishing the 1993 *SOF Posture Statement*, an authoritative guide to SOF missions, programs, and budgetary data. This document has been distributed to Congress, DoD, and the general public.

- Initiating and securing agreement from National Defense University and USSOCOM on creating, funding and filling a SOF faculty chair at NDU beginning in academic year 1993-94. Follow-on activities include establishing official SOF Archives in the Marshall Library and a post-Senior Service College fellowship within the Institute for National Strategic Studies.

- Developing the Ambassador Familiarization Program to acquaint newly appointed ambassadors with military counterterrorist forces. Important topics include the interagency counterterrorism process and military counterterrorism capabilities. This program significantly improved our country's ability to respond appropriately when overseas emergencies occur.

- Initiating and obtaining approval for selected SOF peacetime deployments in support of U.S. foreign policy and taking the lead in developing SOF's role in demining missions.

Procedural Improvements by USSOCOM

Successful special operations depend on esoteric intelligence and a planning, programming, budgeting system that responds to unique needs. USSOCOM has revised old procedures and invented new ones to suit SOF purposes.

Intelligence

Global responsibilities generate unique intelligence requirements for USSOCOM which, unlike geographically oriented combatant commands, must prepare and provide forces ready to perform assigned missions anywhere in the world when so directed. Simultaneous, short-notice deployments to widely separated regions occur routinely. The scope of USSOCOM intelligence accordingly exceeds that of the largest theater. Needs also differ markedly from those of conventional forces.[6]

Further, each SOF mission demands different intelligence support. Foreign internal defense (FID) specialists who hope to prevent insurgencies find political, economic, cultural, and institutional indicators at least as important as military intelligence. Unconventional warfare (UW) experts, vastly outnumbered in enemy territory, must know when to hide and when to attack. Evasion and escape artists need to identify trustworthy contacts, reliable routes, and a string of secure safehouses. Hostage rescue teams demand even more detail: They not only need building floor plans, but must know which way the doors open and the number of stairs in each flight. Special reconnaissance teams, SOF aviation, SEALs, psychological operations, and civil affairs formations also need tailored intelligence.[7]

USSOCOM rated SOF intelligence unsatisfactory in 1987. Input was poor both in quantity and quality. Automated data processing and dedicated communications were nearly nonexistent. Outmoded maps contained large blank sections (many sheets depicted conditions 45 to 50 years ago). Meteorological and oceanographic intelligence were insufficiently specific for detailed SOF planning.[8]

Some intelligence collection, processing, and dissemination deficiencies are beyond USSOCOM control. Interoperability problems, for example, are endemic throughout DoD, and military SOF depend on the Central Intelligence Agency for most human intelligence (HUMINT) support, which remains subject to severe constraints.[9] Even so, U.S. SOF receive more usable intelligence than ever before from national agencies.

USSOCOM's Command Intelligence Architecture Planning Program (CIAP) "has documented in fine detail the intelligence requirements and capabilities...of SOF in all theaters." A Special Operations Command Research, Analysis and Threat Evaluation System (SOCRATES), which incorporates a variety of computers, databases, intelligence communications systems, secure telephones, facsimile equipment, imagery processing/dissemination, and map-handling devices, "provides unprecedented access to national and regional intelligence products...." A man-transportable SOCRATES (MTS) is under development, together with a Special Operations Forces Intelligence Vehicle (SOF-IV) that will permit deployed SOF to "receive, send, process, and analyze near real-time intelligence information." Civilian Multispectral Imagery (MSI) provides USSOCOM with up-to-date map and chart substitutes. Fiber optics and closed circuit TV facilitate secure intelligence tranmissions. A Joint Special Operations Intelligence Course (JSOIC) at the Joint Military Intelligence College in Washington, D.C., puts a SOF-specific slant on assorted subjects that include mission planning, targeting, evasion, escape, recovery, and legal issues.[10]

Prognoses seem bright in most respects, according to the USSOCOM J-2. Interagency cooperation concerning HUMINT is "much better" since Operation *Just Cause* (Panama, 1989-90). USSOCOM is collaborating with all U.S. military services in efforts to prototype and test new, lighter, smaller, interoperable intelligence systems needed for the type conflicts they anticipate. The most important initiatives may reach fruition, because SOF intelligence programs for FY 1993-99 are well supported in the Pentagon and on Capitol Hill, according to the USSOCOM J-2.[11]

Joint Planning-Programming-Budgeting System

The U.S. Special Operations Command created a planning, programming, and budgeting system (PPBS) from scratch. It interlocks with PPBS in the Pentagon, but USSOCOM procedures, unlike those of the Army, Navy, Air Force, and Marine Corps, are joint in every respect.

PPBS currently proceeds in a partial vacuum, because no NSC Board for Low-Intensity Conflict produces overarching policy guidance. The Secretary of Defense recently completed a comprehensive *Bottom-Up Review* of U.S. national military strategy and forces that will reshape SOF plans and programs to unpredictable extents.[12] Budgeteers in the Office of the Secretary of Defense (OSD) have made few provisions for peacetime engagements, such as humanitarian assistance and disaster relief operations that involve recurrent SOF participation. Reiterative USSOCOM PPBS practices, which undergo constant refinement, nevertheless justify as objectively as possible required quantities and characteristics of U.S. Special Operations Forces.

Planning. The USSOCOM planning, programming and budgeting system makes a determination of requirements for total obligation authority and manpower, allocates required resources, requests those resources from Congress, and monitors the application of resources received. Its ultimate objective is to provide "the best mix of forces, equipment, and support attainable within fiscal constraints." Inputs come from Defense Planning Guidance, U.S. national security and national military strategies, the Pentagon's Joint Strategic Planning System, theater CINCs, CINCSOC, the USSOCOM staff, and component commands. Products include a Joint Mission Analysis, a Special Operations Master Plan, and a Long Range Plan.[13]

USSOCOM conducts joint mission analyses in concert with each regionally- oriented unified command to determine "future structure and attributes of Special Operations Forces and to support the Major Force Program (MFP)-11 Program Objective Memorandum."

Analysts, assisted by scenarios and computer models, seek to answer four fundamental questions: how many SOF and supporting airlift/sealift platforms of what sort seem needed to accomplish anticipated missions in specific theaters, sub-regions, countries, and other areas? What forces will be available to satisfy inferred requirements at particular times in the future? What risks result when projected SOF capabilities appear insufficient? What courses of action might reduce those risks, including actions to employ programmed assets more effectively? Joint Mission Analyses ultimately produce a Mission Needs Force that could accomplish all assigned tasks "with a reasonable assurance of success and minimal risk."[14]

The Special Operations Master Plan, which spans both near- and mid-terms (1 to 20 years), attempts to reconcile the fiscally unconstrained Mission Needs Force with budgetary realities. Its aim is "an attainable and properly equipped SOF force structure that supports the National Military Strategy." A Force Structure Board, a Maritime Mobility Board, and a Joint Special Operations Aviation Board review all requirements, sometimes repeatedly.[15]

The Special Operations Long Range Plan seeks to integrate and help direct USSOCOM's short- and mid-range plans with visions of the future 20 to 30 years hence. Because this document reflects political, military, economic, social, environmental, and technological trends that may continue as predicted, terminate, or change unexpectedly, planners must update it continually.[16]

Two senior panels perform "sanity checks" throughout the USSOCOM planning process. Deputy commanders of USSOCOM components constitute a Requirements Review Board (RRB) that convenes quarterly to evaluate new or revised requirements, relate them to missions, and put them in priority. The RRB semiannually submits its findings to a Requirements Oversight Council (ROC), whose members include CINCSOC and all component commanders. The Objective Force that the CINC finally approves constitutes the starting point for USSOCOM programs and budget estimates.[17]

The current Objective Force at first glance seems inconsistent with ongoing efforts to reduce the U.S military establishment and defense budget. Active SOF personnel strengths continue to climb, as do inventories of costly weapon systems, most notably HC-130 Combat Shadows, MC-130 Combat Talons, MH-53 Pave Low helicopters, and Cyclone Class coastal patrol ships.[18] Conversely, conventional forces in all U.S. Armed Forces have been declining since the Soviet Union and Warsaw pact collapsed. Two conditions explain that anomaly, according to spokesmen in Headquarters, USSOCOM and in component commands: Most U.S. conventional forces were deployed primarily to deal with Soviet threats during the Cold War, while most multipurpose SOF served diversified purposes. U.S. Special Operations Forces still are trying to recover from the lengthy period of neglect that caused Congress to enact remedial legislation in 1986.[19]

Programming. USSOCOM programmers convert CINCSOC's Objective Force into a Program Objective Memorandum (POM) that covers 6 years beyond current budget years. Each element of that proposal relates a specific combat or support force category, manpower, and cost figures with objectives to be achieved. The process links Major Force Program (MFP)-11, which covers special operations-peculiar equipment, with other programs that contribute to USSOCOM's capabilities.[20]

When programming cycles begin, CINCSOC has opportunities to influence DoD's draft Defense Guidance through written and oral comments and also to contribute to an Integrated Priority List that biannually tells the Secretary of Defense and Chairman of the Joint Chiefs of Staff which programs are considered most important. Component commands, including their schools, provide input. They thereafter submit their respective MFP-11 program requests to USSOCOM; non-MFP-11 requests go directly to Military Departments (Army, Navy, Air Force), which furnish common weapons, equipment, supplies, and services that are not "special operations-peculiar."[21]

The USSOCOM corporate review system for PPBS consists of three panels (mobility, support, special access), a military construction board, an Executive Committee (EXCOM), and a Joint Program Review Board (JPRB). The EXCOM, co-chaired by the USSOCOM J-8 and ASD SO/LIC Director of Requirements and Programs, integrates all programming actions. The Deputy Commander in Chief of USSOCOM and Principal Deputy Assistant Secretary of Defense (SO/LIC) co-chair the JPRB, which evaluates EXCOM recommendations before CINCSOC approves or disapproves. The ASD SO/LIC staff participates at every working level throughout the PPBS process.[22]

Budgeting. CINCSOC first exercised authority for MFP-11

programs with the submission of the FY 1991 President's Budget. The Assistant Secretary of Defense for Program Analysis and Evaluation (ASD PA&E), however, determines what USSOCOM can afford in its budget. OSD establishes the financial baseline for USSOCOM's Program Objective Memorandum, then issues further guidance via the Program Decision Memorandum, which establishes the baseline for USSOCOM's Budget Estimate Submission.[23] SOCOM follows budgeting procedures delineated in the Department of Defense Budget Guidance Manual (DoD Manual 7110-1-M) and associated policy memos issued periodically by the DoD Comptroller. Those documents provide basic references for the preparation, justification, and execution of budget requirements within the Department of Defense. USSOCOM also maintains a Policy Book which interprets and further refines DoD's guidance.[24]

ASD SO/LIC reviews USSOCOM's Budget Estimate Submission before it reaches the OSD Comptroller. Draft Program Budget Decisions that flow therefrom affect Major Force Program-11, USSOCOM, and the Services. The Defense Planning Resource Board, with CINCSOC present, debates unresolved disagreements and addresses USSOCOM requirements that MFP-11 does not cover. Final Program Budget Decisions follow. The ASD SO/LIC and CINCSOC annually defend USSOCOM portions of the President's budget before Congress. OSD issues MFP-11 funds to USSOCOM after Congress approves and the President signs authorization/appropriation acts. USSOCOM then issues fund authorizations to the services so they can execute Major Force Program-11 and oversees the execution during Summer Budget Reviews. The process begins anew for each fiscal year.[25]

Force Posture Improvements

Force posture improvements since 1986 occupy two categories: Some beneficial trends apply equally to the entire SOF community, others affect each component command and theater SOC somewhat differently.

Overarching Developments

Better arms, equipment, personnel, and integrating structures are evident everywhere in USSOCOM and among Special Operations Forces in all overseas unified commands. Concentrated education and training help commanders make the most of available assets.

Force structure. SOF force structure began to thrive soon after congressional legislation encouraged growth. Controlling headquarters sprouted or expanded: USSOCOM at MacDill AFB, FL; U.S. Army Special Operations Command (USASOC) at Fort Bragg, NC; Naval Special Warfare Command (NAVSPECWARCOM) at Coronado, CA; and Air Force Special Operations Command (AFSOC) at Hurlburt Field, FL. Each component added active units that embellish uniservice and joint capabilities (table 1). USASOC shows the greatest gains, but all augmentations are significant.

Revitalization continues at modest cost compared with funds for conventional forces. FY 1994 budget requests for SOF procurement, personnel, operations, maintenance, research, development, test, evaluation, and military construction comprised little more than one penny out of every DoD dollar.[26]

Personnel Management. Past and present Commanders in Chief of U.S. Special Operations Command all believe that SOF personnel are more important than hardware, that their qualities are more important than quantities, and that they cannot be mass produced or created after emergencies occur. CINCSOCs also feel, and their senior subordinates agree, that putting the right people in the right places is the key to successful mission accomplishment.

USSOCOM and its component commands "must have a carefully thought out personnel management plan," according to General Stiner, because "we do not, and will not for the foreseeable future, have enough fully qualified, articulate SOF personnel to fill all the positions that call for people with SOF expertise." Strict professionalism is the top priority. USSOCOM and its components work hard to eradicate misperceptions that Rambo-style "snake eaters [and] reckless, out-of-control individuals who worked for their own ends often against the policies of established authority" typify special operations personnel.[27] He considers that image intolerable, "because "discipline and maturity are part of what makes us special."[28]

All Army and Navy SOF are volunteers. Most demonstrate superior performance during tours with conventional forces before they convert. Recruiting practices vary with each parent service (the Navy, for example, takes some prospective SEALs straight from basic training, Army Special Forces do not), but standards are uniformly

Table 1. *SOF force structure growth, 1986-1993*

Year	ARMY	AIR FORCE	NAVY	JOINT
	Active Forces			
1986	1st SOCOM # (4) SF Groups PSYOP Grp. Ranger Rgt. CA Bn. Aviation Group # Aviation Co. # Signal Bn.(-)	23rd AF HQs. # SO Wing HQs. (5) SO Sqs.	(2) NSWG HQs. (3) NSWUs. (5) SEAL Teams (2) SDV Teams (2) Special Boat Sq. HQs. (2) Special Boat Units	SOCEUR HQs. SOCPAC HQs. SOCCENT HQs. SOCSOUTH HQs. SOCLANT HQs. JSOC HQs. JSOA #
	Reserve Forces			
1986	(2) NG SF Grps. (2) AR SF Grps. (3) AR PSYOP Grps (8) AR CA Cmds/Bdes. NG Aviation Bn.	(2) AFR SO Sqs. ANG SO Sq.	(4) NR Special Boat Units (8) NR NSW Dets.	
	Force Changes Since 1987:			
1987	Support Bn. Aviation Det.	Special Tactics Grp.	NAVSPECWARCOM HQs. Special Boat Unit	USSOCOM HQs. JCS J3-SOD
1988			NSWU SEAL Team	
1989	USASOC HQs. Aviation Rgt. HQs Aviation Bn.	(2) SO Grp. HQs. (6) SO Sqs.		
1990	SF Group (-) (5) TASOSCs	AFSOC HQs.		
1991	SF Cmd HQs. CAPOC HQs. SF Bn.			
1992	SF Bn.			
1993			(2) Submarine Conversions	

Note: # indicates that unit was later eliminated or absorbed by another activity.
      (-) indicates unit activation at partial strength.

Note: See appendix D for abbreviations

high.[29] Retention requirements also are stringent. Recalcitrants rarely last long.[30]

   Weapons and equipment. Defense publications in the mid-1980s deplored special operations hardware deficiencies. "We've got bands that are in a higher state of readiness than some of our special operations assets," is the way one Pentagon official put it.[31] DoD and Congress validated needs, but few funds were forthcoming.

   SOF airlift, sealift, and communications in particular require special research, development, and procurement programs, but all got short shrift before 1986. Fixed- and rotary-wing SOF aircraft inventories in 1985 included 13 MC-130 Combat Talons and 7 HH-53 Pave Low helicopters. All 11 aircraft ordered into the air during an Operational Readiness Inspection at Hurlburt Field, FL, in each will be able to embark a pair of SEAL Delivery Vehicles in dry deck shelters. December 1985 flunked the test.[32] "Many SEALs and virtually all Special Forces troopers [went] through their careers making amphibious insertions from short-range boats or Coast Guard cutters," because both Vietnam War vintage SOF submarines had been decommissioned. AN/PRC-70 "portable" radios weighed 45 pounds, and their batteries drained so rapidly that replacements increased that load considerably. Repair parts were in short supply. Television sets aboard Air National Guard Coronet Solo EC-130 PSYOP aircraft could broadcast to receivers in North and Central America, but required extensive conversion for use anywhere else in the world.[33]

   Most such deficiencies have been corrected. Six Air Force aircraft programs currently are in progress. Combat Talons and Pave Low helicopters now number 28 and 41, respectively; the Army's Special Operations Aviation Regiment is receiving updated MH-60 Black Hawk and MH-47 Chinook helicopters; new model AC-130 Spectre gunships and improved munitions will deploy before long; and two POLARIS class ballistic missile submarines, each able to embark a pair of SEAL Delivery Vehicles in dry deck shelters, soon will complete conversion to SOF troop carriers. A Joint Advanced Special Operations Radio System (JASORs) that features a family of radios and associated equipment is in development. Enhanced tactical radio and television systems able to broadcast, record, and retransmit material to enhance PSYOP/civil affairs capabilities are undergoing operational test, evaluation, and continued production. Special operations specific hardware with other applications also is making progress.[34]

Unit Readiness. Combat readiness was the "number one priority" of USSOCOM when General Stiner was CINCSOC and remains so today. Well-armed, well-equipped, well-supplied, highly motivated professionals are essential, but proficient units are even more important than skilled individuals. Superior education and training at all levels thus are key requirements.[35]

USSOCOM operates its own school system. The John F. Kennedy Special Warfare Center and School at Fort Bragg, NC, develops doctrine and conducts courses for all Army SOF and Foreign Area Officers (FAO). The Naval Special Warfare Center at the Naval Amphibious Base, Coronado, CA, and the U.S. Air Force Special Operations School at Hurlburt Field, FL, do likewise within respective spheres. All three instruct foreign students as well as personnel from non-DoD departments and agencies. A Joint Schools Integration Committee, which consists of USSOCOM's Deputy J-3 and the three school commandants, has met quarterly since 1987 to coordinate curricula and avoid undesirable redundancy. As a direct result, the JFK Center and School conducts language training for SOF regardless of Service. A Special Operations Medical Training Center at Fort Bragg, currently under construction, will consolidate SOF medical instruction at considerable savings in duplicative structures, travel times, and costs.[36]

Intensive, extensive, and diversified courses of instruction cover a wide range of subjects and scenarios. Members of small, self-contained teams concentrate on cross-training (e.g., demolition experts may not become fully proficient as radio operators or medics, but must be qualified to perform such duties in emergency). USSOCOM also cultivates linguistic and cross-cultural skills, which many SOF need to accomplish regional security missions in an ever more complex world. Conventional units do not match their competence.[37]

Readiness · varies considerably. Finely honed forces that specialize in counterterrorism, direct action, and strategic reconnaissance are prepared to move anywhere in the world almost on moment's notice. USSOCOM is less able to provide SOF that are fluent in required foreign languages and otherwise well prepared to establish essential relationships in countries like Bosnia-Hercegovina. Special Operations Forces from all services nevertheless have repeatedly answered calls for help in Kurdistan, Somalia, and other out-of-the-way places since 1990. Most, but not all, results have been admirable.[38]

Logistics. The U.S. Army, Navy, and Air Force furnished all logistic support for SOF before Congress created USSOCOM. They still provide common weapons, equipment, supplies, and services, but a Special Operations Forces Support Activity (SOFSA) outside Lexington, KY has handled low-density, SOF-peculiar needs for Army forces since 1988. The Joint Operational Stocks (JOS) Program, a centrally managed repository of some SOF-specific hardware, is collocated.[39]

SOFSA is a government-owned, contractor-operated facility that maintains, repairs, and modifies SOF-specific items. Typical functions include fabrication, reconfiguration, systems integration, purchasing, requisitioning, direct exchange, and routine logistic support. SOFSA also deploys maintenance teams on request. It eventually will accumulate contingency stocks for USSOCOM if DoD approves proposals and Congress appropriates funds. SOFSA accepts non-SOF customers and charges only for work performed to keep costs low. The contractor must flex his work force to meet fluctuating demands or pay for excess capacities out of his own pocket.[40]

The Joint Operational Stocks Program procures small quantities of SOF-peculiar items that are then issued temporarily to theater SOCs and USSOCOM component commands for training and operational purposes. Borrowers return all items when missions are complete. Stocks feature civilian products that have military applications and demand minimum familiarization before use. Off-the-shelf purchases reduce needs for research, development, test, or evaluation funds. Anticipated utility of most stocks averages about three years.[41]

Army Component Command

U.S. Army Special Operations Command (USASOC), activated at Fort Bragg, NC, on 1 December 1989 as an Army Major Command, controls all active Army and Army Reserve SOF in the Continental United States and transmits policy guidance to National Guard units through state adjutants general. The Commanding General wears three stars, up one from the predecessor. USASOC also provides a rotation base for all Army Special Operations Forces overseas.

1. General Wayne A. Downing, Commander in Chief, U.S. Special Operations Command, May 1993 to present.

2. General Carl W. Stiner, Commander in Chief, U.S. Special Operations Command, June 1990-May 1993.

3. General James J. Lindsay, Commander in Chief, U.S. Special Operations Command, June 1987-May 1990.

4. Rangers fast rope from a hovering Air Force MH-53 Pave Low helicopter.

5. Army Special Forces oriented on Europe are skilled at alpine warfare.

6. MC-130 Combat Talon crews are unsurpassed at low-level flight under blackout conditions.

7. SEALs approach the shore in a light inflatable boat (IBS).

8. A SEAL patrol debarks from a miniarmored troop carrier (MATC).

9. Army MH-6 "Little Birds" pack a tremendous punch despite their small size.

10. Rangers roll off a C-130 on all-terrain vehicles.

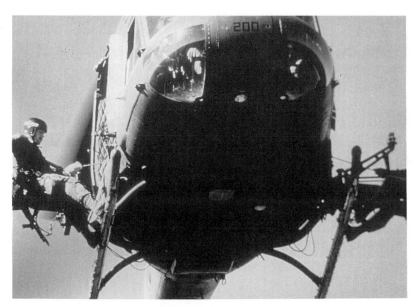

11. "Snipers" on "Little Bird" skids prepare to pick off simulated enemy personnel.

12. Instruction for foreign armed forces is an Army Special Forces specialty.

13. Firepower aboard AC-130H Spectre gunships includes a 105-mm cannon with beacon-tracking radar.

14. A combat swimmer armed with a Hechler and Koch suppressed submachine gun commences operations ashore.

15. SEALs emerge from the sea to begin a beach reconnaissance.

16. An AC-130 Spectre gunship engages hostile forces with one of its 40-mm cannons.

17. U.S. Special Operations Forces assist refugees.

Subordinates include a new Special Forces Command formed on 27 November 1990, a new Civil Affairs and Psychological Operations Command activated simultaneously, and an Integration Command that administratively oversees the Ranger Regiment and Special Operations Aviation Regiment. The John F. Kennedy Special Warfare Center and School has been under USASOC's purview since 20 June 1990, when the Army Training and Doctrine Command relinquished control (see figure 2).[42] Total personnel strength, active and reserve, is about 30,000.

CINCSOC and the Army Chief of Staff have concluded a Memorandum of Agreement (MOA) regarding responsibilities. The basic document addresses 17 topics: recruiting; force development; mobilization-deployment, redeployment-demobilization; training; property acquisition, construction, maintenance, and repair of infrastructure; supply and sustainment; equipping, including R & D; supervision and control of intelligence activities; management of Major Force Program 11; budget preparation and execution; specialty proponency and professional development; combatting terrorism; administration; legal support; transfer of classified programs; command, control, communications, and intelligence (C^3I) special project support; and the management of special access programs. The MOA and all annexes are subject to biennial review and updating as required.[43]

Special Forces Command. Special Forces Command (USASFC), the largest USASOC component, consists of five active Special Forces groups, two in the U.S. Army Reserve (USAR), two more in the Army National Guard (ARNG), a signal battalion, and a support battalion. The authorized strength of each group exceeds 1,400 personnel. The 3d Special Forces Group, oriented on Africa, the signal battalion, and the support battalion have been activated at Fort Bragg since 1986.[44]

Special Forces became a separate combat arms branch of the U.S. Army, analogous to infantry, armor, and artillery, on 9 April 1987. The new branch is experiencing "growing pains" (spaces outnumber faces and personnel management problems must yet be surmounted), but it provides a "home" for Special Forces officers.[45] A stringent assessment and selection process, instituted in 1988, weeds out about half of all volunteers. That preliminary winnowing reduces attrition and thereby cuts costs during a highly competitive qualification course which eliminates another 15 percent.[46]

Figure 2. *Army Special Operations Command*

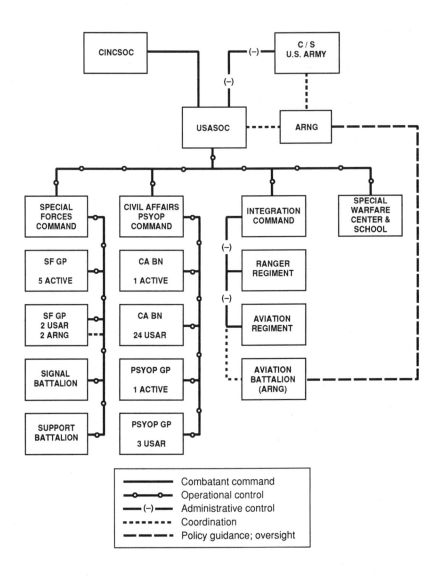

Note: See appendix D for abbreviations

Professional development programs, "the cornerstone for unit leader training," embrace formal schooling, informal discussions, counseling sessions, and progressive assignments, all keyed to a Mission Essential Task List. Unit training concentrates on theater CINC/SOC mission requirements, integration of Special Forces with conventional forces, and language training. USASFC annually participates in many joint exercises at home. Its troops also interacted with armed forces of 17 foreign countries during the last half of 1992. Its commanding general identified superior personnel and capable detachments as solid strengths early in 1993. Area orientation, language qualifications, and communications equipment still need improvement.[47]

Integration Command. A recently formed Integration Command, with the USASOC Deputy Commanding General in charge, exercises command authority less operational control over all Army Rangers and special operations aviation forces stationed in the Continental United States (CINCSOC retains operational control). It also oversees and evaluates training of special operations aviation in the Army National Guard.[48]

U.S. Army Rangers possess a proud tradition.[49] The present organization, with an authorized strength of 1,868 volunteers, consists of a regimental headquarters and one battalion at Fort Benning, GA, a battalion at Fort Stewart, GA, and a battalion at Fort Lewis, WA. That structure was in place by October 1984, but the Ranger Regiment now is much improved in several important respects. Many enlisted Rangers, like other SOF, are college caliber (some accept discharges, complete their education, and return as officers). Individual/unit training has intensified (ammunition expenditure alone far exceeds that of regular infantry). Exercises with other U.S. SOF and conventional forces, as well as with foreigners, has significantly increased. The 75th Ranger Regiment consequently is "fully prepared" to execute all essential missions, according to its commander.[50]

The 160th Special Operations Aviation Regiment (SOAR), which bases two active duty battalions at Fort Campbell, KY, and one at Hunter Army Airfield, GA, replaced a group of the same designation on 16 May 1990. One Oklahoma ARNG battalion is affiliated. Authorized personnel total 1,396. Assigned helicopters include MH-60 Black Hawks, MH-47 Chinooks, and A/MH-6 "Little Birds." Missions range from infiltration, resupply, and exfiltration support for

Special Forces, SEALs, and Rangers to armed attack, aerial security, medical evacuation, electronic warfare, mine dispersal, and command/control. The five top operational priorities are aviation support for Special Mission Units; JCS and CINC directed exercises; SOF selection/training; joint training; support for the National Training Center, Joint Readiness Training Center, and Combined Maneuver Training Center (the latter is in Germany). SOAR pilots and crews are helping Air Force SOF "rewrite the book" on night flying; some have logged 1,000 to 2,000 hours wearing night-vision goggles. The SOAR Commander reports that "the 160th is combat ready."[51]

Civil Affairs and Psychological Operations Command. The Department of the Army approved a career management field for civil affairs and psychological operations in 1988. On 3 March 1993 the Secretary of Defense officially designated as Special Operations Forces "all Psychological Operations and Civil Affairs forces currently assigned to the U.S. Special Operations Command...," although CA and PSYOP units assist conventional forces more often than they support SOF. The U.S. Army Civil Affairs and Psychological Operations Command (USACAPOC) commands the lot, including three civil affairs commands and three PSYOP groups in the USAR.[52]

The 96th Civil Affairs Battalion, authorized 212 officers and enlisted personnel, resides at Fort Bragg, NC. Twenty-four more battalions are in the U.S. Army Reserve, a repository for CA skills that the lone active battalion cannot replicate (typical specialties include public administration, education, finance, health, safety, welfare, labor relations, legal matters, property control, transportation, food distribution, and public works). Sixteen USAR units and selected individuals participated in Operations *Desert Shield/Storm,* but reserves are not readily available for peacetime missions that have multiplied rapidly around the world since the Cold War ended. The 96th CA Battalion accordingly is fully occupied, with few breathing spells. There is little margin for mistakes, because television cameras capture every CA move and bobbles could embarrass the U.S. Government.[53]

One active duty psychological operations group with an authorized strength of 1,137 personnel is based at Fort Bragg. Three of its five battalions are regionally oriented; the remainder reinforce and otherwise support as required. Three PSYOP groups in the U.S.

Army Reserve constitute backup. CINCSOC and the U.S. Army Special Operations Command seem to have helped PSYOP units contribute more effectively than they did when control was decentralized. PSYOP proved to be a classic force multiplier during war with Iraq in 1990-91. Less publicized applications that, for example, helped explain U.S. activities in Somalia have more recently been effective behind the scenes.[54]

JFK Special Warfare Center and School. The John F. Kennedy Special Warfare Center and School (JFKSWCS) is a direct descendant of the Psychological Warfare Center that the U.S. Army established at Fort Bragg, NC, in 1952. The major general in command pursues a twofold mission: To develop special operations doctrine for USASOC and the Army at large, and to provide entry level and advanced training for Army Special Forces, Civil Affairs, and PSYOP forces.[55]

Two doctrinal developments have significantly altered procedures since 1986. The JFK Center received concept approval in 1988 to establish Theater Army Special Operations Support Commands (TASOSCs) designed to improve combat service support for U.S. forward-deployed SOF. The Center and XVIII Airborne Corps began to test a Special Operations Coordination Element (SOCOORD) that same year. The April 1990 edition of Army Field Manual (FM) 31-20, *Doctrine for Special Forces*, calls for every corps planning staff to incorporate a SOCOORD cell consisting of one lieutenant colonel, a major, a captain, and a sergeant major who are Special Forces or Ranger qualified. Their purpose is to help synchronize conventional and special operations within corps areas of interest and responsibility.[56]

The JFK School conducts more than 30 courses for students from active U.S. Army, USAR, and ARNG units. Interservice and foreign students average about 700 per year. Basic instruction emphasizes tactics, weapons, communications, medical, and special operations engineering skills, with attention to such subjects as sniper training; sabotage techniques; survival, evasion, resistance, and escape (SERE); burst radio operation; and free-fall parachuting. Advanced education and training features regional studies, cross-cultural understanding, foreign internal defense, and foreign language courses.[57]

A Special Operations Staff Officer course opened in 1988. Soon thereafter, the JFK Center and School activated a Special Warfare Training Group to consolidate management functions. The 1st

Battalion conducts Special Forces assessment, selection, and qualification courses. The 2d Battalion handles advanced specialties that include HALO/HAHO (high-altitude, low-opening, high-altitude, high-opening) parachute techniques and counterterrorism training. Civil affairs and psychological operations are 3d Battalion responsibilities.[58]

The JFKSWCS Commander believes that unit training is producing the "best level of readiness to date." Foreign language proficiency remains the main deficiency, especially among Reserve Component SOF. PSYOP groups find it particularly difficult to score high readiness marks, given new criteria that increase language requirements by 79 percent.[59]

Air Force Component Command

Air Force SOF (AFSOF) were badly debilitated after drawdowns that followed the Vietnam War. Those years "were marked by controversy, inter-service and intra-Air Force rivalries, jealousies, [and] frequent disruptive reorganizations," according to a now-retired general officer. Most pilots and crews considered the 1 March 1983 transfer from Tactical Air Command (TAC) to Military Airlift Command (MAC) "a definite step down and an indicator that the [Air Force] leadership viewed them as 'trash haulers' and combat supporters, not leading edge, point of the spear, warriors."[60]

Needs for reconfiguration, refurbishment, and revitalization were apparent before Congress enacted corrective legislation in 1986, because virtually every U.S. special operation requires AFSOF participation with other SOF, conventional forces, and/or foreign military formations. AFSOF provide airlift for insertion, support, and extraction; perform economy of force missions; "surgically" attack sensitive targets beyond the capabilities of or inappropriate for fighter aircraft or bombers (such as nuclear, chemical, and biological installations collocated with civilians); assist escape, rescue, and SOF recovery operations; and facilitate PSYOP.[61]

Reconfiguration. When USSOCOM was activated in April 1987, all AFSOF belonged to 23d Air Force, a subordinate of Military Airlift Command. Clean command relationships remained elusive for nearly 3 years until an Air Force Special Operations Command (AFSOC) replaced 23d Air Force in May 1990, severed all ties with MAC, and became a Major Command of the USAF.[62]   A

Memorandum of Agreement between CINCSOC and the USAF Chief of Staff, reviewed biennially and updated as required, describes respective duties.[63]

The AFSOC Commander, who wears two stars, commands one active and one Air Force Reserve (AFRES) composite wing that contain fixed- and rotary-wing squadrons. A Special Tactics Group (STG), a Special Missions Operational Test and Evaluation Center (SMOTEC), the USAF Special Operations School (USAFSOS), and ownership of Hurlburt Field complete AFSOC's stateside structure. Military and civilian personnel total about 6,600 at Hurlburt Field and Eglin AFB, FL. AFSOC additionally transmits policy guidance to a special operations group in the Air National Guard (ANG). It also furnishes forces to and provides a rotation base for two U.S. special operations commands overseas: one group in England serves CINCEUR; another in Japan and Korea serves CINCPAC (figure 3).[64] All aforementioned organizations except the Special Tactics Group predate 1986, but weapons, equipment, tactics, and techniques have subsequently been improved.

Refurbishment. AFSOF have refurbished rapidly, despite schedule slippages and cost overruns in MC-130H and AC-130U programs.[65] The most sophisticated aircraft, once in very short supply, now (or soon will) match numbers the Chairman of the Joint Chiefs of Staff and Deputy Secretary of Defense recommended in 1986 (table 2).[66]

One squadron of the 1st Special Operations Wing (SOW) at Hurlburt Field, a squadron at Alconbury, England, and a squadron at Kadena Air Base, Japan, fly multipurpose Combat Talons that are designed to conduct clandestine, low-level night infiltration, exfiltration, resupply, PSYOP, and aerial reconnaissance missions over all types of terrain deep in enemy territory. All can deliver troops, equipment, and supplies onto short landing strips or small drop zones. Some come equipped with surface-to-air recovery (STAR) systems. Combat Talons II have a larger cargo capacity than Talon I and, when computer power "glitches" are corrected, will possess much better radars. Planned deployments will total 24 in October 1994, if prognoses prove correct.[67]

16th SOW flies air refuelable AC-130H Spectre gunships armed with twin 20-mm cannons, a 40-mm cannon, and one 105-mm howitzer which make formidable weapons for close air support, air interdiction, and armed reconnaissance. Electronic warfare, infrared

Figure 3. *Air Force Special Operations Command*

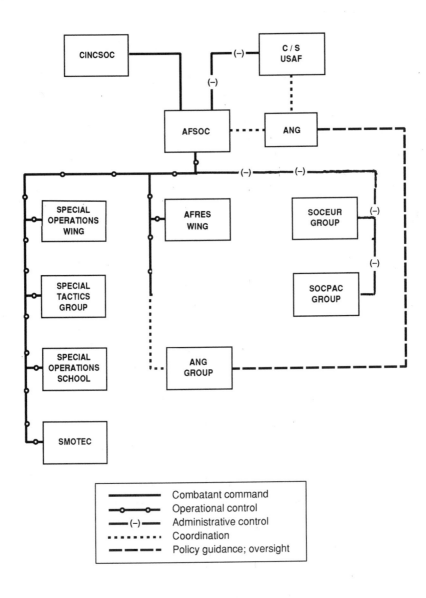

Note: See appendix D for abbreviations

defense, and target acquisition suites are equally impressive. A searchlight, low light level television, battlefield illumination flares, and infrared sensors, together with hi-tech navigation and fire control systems, facilitate pinpoint accuracy during extended loiter periods at night and in adverse weather. An AF Reserve squadron at Duke Field, FL, possesses AC-130A models armed with two 40-mm cannons, two 20- mm gatling cannons, and two 7.62-mm mini-guns, but no howitzer. AC-130Us, which pack somewhat more punch at longer ranges and boast much better all-weather attack capabilities, currently are undergoing flight tests. AFSOC plans to procure 13, transfer all AC-130Hs to the Air Force Reserve, and retire all AC-130A models by September 1995.[68]

One HC-130P/N Combat Shadow squadron at Eglin AFB, FL, stands ready to refuel U.S.-based Army and AFSOF helicopters in flight. Two other squadrons at Alconbury and Kadena perform identical functions for SOCEUR and SOCPAC. Upgrades are in progress, but Combat Shadows nevertheless will remain best reserved for operations in relatively low-threat environments, because they lack terrain-following radars and state-of-the art countermeasures. Combat Talons I are better suited to fly low-level refueling missions at night during foul weather in high threat regions where topographic obstacles abound.[69]

An Air National Guard special operations group at Harrisburg Airport, PA, operates four EC-130E Commando Solos, the only aircraft dedicated exclusively to PSYOP. They can broadcast over AM, FM, and HF radio bands and beam color television programs via VHF/UHF.[70]

The USAF possessed just seven MH-53H Pave Low helicopters in 1986. AFSOC now owns 41 much improved "J" models, the world's most technologically advanced rotary-wing aircraft. Fourteen are shipboard capable; the remainder are scheduled to receive required upgrades. No other helicopter can match their abilities to penetrate deeply into hostile or denied air space during foul weather in the dead of night and return undetected. In-flight refueling limits range primarily to aircrew endurance. Active and passive defenses include three 7.62-mm mini-guns or three .50-caliber machine guns, armor plating, and assorted electronic countermeasures. Interactive Defensive Avionics Suite (IDAS) and Multi Advanced Tactical Terminal (MATT) programs designed to detect and help defeat threats are undergoing development. The 1st Special Operations

Table 2. *AFSOC aircraft inventories*

		1986 inventory	Proposed inventory	June 1993 inventory
CV-22	Osprey	0	55	0
MC-130E	Combat Talon	14	14	14
MC-130H	Combat Talon II	0	24	14
AC-130A	Spectre Gunship	10	10	10
AC-130H	Spectre Gunship	10	10	9
AC-130U	Spectre Gunship	0	13	0
HC-130P/N	Combat Shadow	31	31	28
EC-130E	Commando Solo	4	6	4
MH-53	Pave Low	7	35	41
MH-60G	Pave Hawk	<u>10</u>	<u>10</u>	<u>10</u>
		86	208	130

Wing, SOCEUR, and SOCPAC all employ MH-53Js for clandestine infiltration, exfiltration, resupply, and (sometimes) medical evacuationpurposes. Each helicopter can transport 37 fully equipped troops or 16 litters.[71]

A special operations squadron at Hurlburt Field flies all 10 of AFSOC's MH-60G Pave Hawk helicopters, which receive missions similar to those of Pave Lows but carry smaller loads and fewer troops. Folding rotor blades and tail stabilators facilitate shipboard operations and transportability by C-5A aircraft. New navigation equipment and engine modifications will enhance present performance considerably.[72]

The Special Missions Operational Test and Evaluation Center (SMOTEC), headquartered at Hurlburt Field, examines all AFSOC aircraft types/models/modifications and weapon systems to determine suitability before deployment. The six-division test squadron at Edwards AFB, CA, furnishes fixed-wing, rotary-wing, Combat Talon II, electronic combat, operational analysis, and operations support. The 18th Test Squadron, a subordinate unit, evaluates the AC-130U.[73]

AFSOC veterans recall December 1985, when all 11 aircraft being tested at Hurlburt Field failed to pass a routine Operational Readiness Test.[74] Launch reliability rates during Operation *Desert Storm* approximated 99 percent for all aircraft, according to AFSOC reports, despite blistering heat and blowing sand that made maintenance a nightmare. Air commandos who fly and support every mission are justifiably proud of that record. AFSOC, in short, "has never been as ready for a contingency as it is today," according to its Commander.[75]

Revitalization. One of AFSOF's six basic objectives is to "build and maintain a respected force of highly motivated and qualified people." Contributing aims focus on efforts to recruit, select, retain, and professionally develop first-class commissioned and noncommissioned officers.[76] Progress is apparent.

Many AFSOC members, including some senior officers, are part-time SOF and part-time conventional airmen. That situation is slowly improving. Aircrew selection criteria, for example, cull unfit applicants before rigorous, costly, time-consuming training begins. The Special Tactics Group fills combat controller and paramedic slots only after candidates successfully complete a 9-week evaluation/indoctrination course emphasizing physical and psychological fitness of the first order (80 percent usually fail; the remainder win wings).[77]

The promotion potential of AFSOC master sergeants, majors, lieutenant colonels, and colonels has been as good or better than in the conventional Air Force and among other SOF since 1991. Officers eligible to attend intermediate and senior service colleges likewise find pleasant prospects. Retention rates for aircrews currently are high: fixed-wing pilots, 85 percent; rotary-wing pilots, 94 percent. First-term and career reenlistment rates among men and women in the ranks equal or exceed Air Force averages.[78]

The USAF Special Operations School, unlike Army and Navy counterparts, emphasizes education rather than training. Three thousand resident students from the U.S. SOF community, the U.S. military services, and foreign countries graduate annually. The school offers 15 short courses (3 to 10 days each) 72 times per year. They cover a broad spectrum of subjects, to include cross-cultural communications, revolutionary warfare, foreign internal defense, crisis response management, psychological operations, and area orientations.[79]

Navy Component Command

The Naval Special Warfare Command (NAVSPECWARCOM) was established 16 April 1987 in Coronado, CA.[80] Its mission, somewhat expanded since 1987, is to organize, equip, train, and provide naval SOF that specialize in maritime and riverine operations. Foreign internal defense (FID) enjoys top priority in peacetime. Direct action is the main combat mission. NAVSPECWARCOM also provides maritime mobility for SOF from other services.[81]

The one-star admiral who commands NAVSPECWARCOM has exercised operational control over all U.S.-based Naval Special Warfare (NSW) forces since March 1988, shortly after the Secretary of Defense disapproved dissents by senior Navy officials[82] (one SEAL team permanently assigned to USSOCOM's Special Mission Units is the sole exception). As of October 1988, the Commander of NAVSPECWARCOM also has been responsible for the administration, training, maintenance, support, and readiness of all active NSW forces, including those assigned to unified commands overseas. The Naval Surface Reserve Force administers and supports NSW reserves.

Total active and reserve personnel strength of NAVSPECWARCOM approximates 5,500. Naval Special Warfare Group One in Coronado, CA, and Group Two at Little Creek, VA, each contain three SEAL teams and a SEAL Delivery Vehicle (SDV) team (figure 4). Two special boat squadrons became separate major commands in 1993. A Naval Special Warfare Center, collocated with NAVSPECWARCOM on the Amphibious Base in Coronado, is the NSW "schoolhouse" and source of new doctrine. A Naval Special Warfare Development Group, activated at Little Creek in September 1989, provides centralized management for the development, test, and evaluation of current and emerging technologies that might have

Figure 4. *Naval Special Warfare Command*

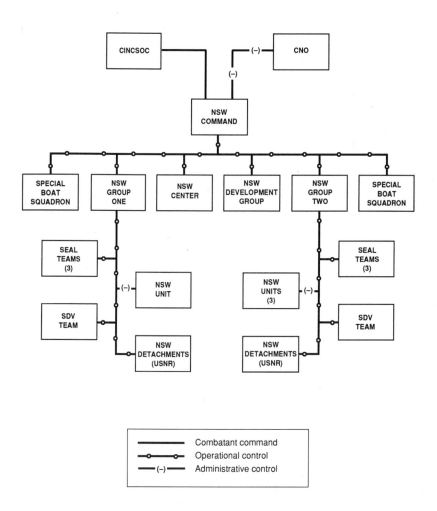

Note: See appendix D for abbreviations

NSW applications. It also devises maritime, ground, and airborne tactics.[83]

NSW Unit One, based on Guam, has five SEAL platoons and a Special Boat Unit assigned. Seventh Fleet exercises operational control over all except one SEAL platoon, which Special Operations Command, Pacific controls. Special Operations Command, Europe has operational control over NSW Unit Two. Two SEAL platoons, their boat detachments, and an SDV Task Unit are U.S. Sixth Fleet assets in the Mediterranean. U.S. Atlantic Fleet Detachment South exercises operational control over NSW Unit Eight, which bases two SEAL platoons and a Special Boat Unit in Panama, but coordinates all activities with SOCSOUTH. The NAVSPECWARCOM Commander negotiated four Memoranda of Agreement (MOA) between May and October 1988 to ensure proper support for NSW deployed forces and for the Naval Special Warfare Center. Other signatories were CINCLANT Fleet; CINCPAC Fleet; Commander, Submarine Force Pacific; and the Chief of Naval Education and Training. CINCSOC and the Chief of Naval Operations subsequently concluded a more comprehensive MOA.[84]

SEAL Teams. Highly mobile, lightly armed SEAL teams, sharply reduced after the Vietnam War, have revived. Only one new team has been activated since 1986, but the number of 16-man platoons is now 60, compared with fewer than 20 as late as 1981. Each relies on concealment and surprise to accomplish most combat missions, which include unconventional warfare, foreign internal defense, counterterrorism, direct action, and special reconnaissance. Hydrographic/coastal intelligence, underwater demolition, raids, combat swimming, and riverine operations are SEAL specialties.[85]

Assessment and acceptance standards are stringent. Each aspirant must conclude 7 weeks of preconditioning and indoctrination before beginning the 6-month Basic Underwater Demolition/SEAL (BUD/S) course that the Navel Special Warfare Center conducts in Coronado, CA. Basic parachute training follows at Fort Benning, GA. Survivors win coveted insignia only after they successfully complete a 6-month probationary period with a SEAL or SDV team.[86]

Twelve SEAL platoons are always forward deployed on 6-month tours for use as regional commanders see fit. Twelve more SEAL platoons engage in predeployment training for 6 months, another dozen perform post-deployment tasks (such as maintenance), take advanced individual training (such as military freefall parachuting and maritime operations), rest, and recuperate. Among the remaining 24 platoons, two in each team act as training cells on a rotational basis. Twelve participate in exercises, on military training teams, and are otherwise employed in bilateral exhanges with foreign counterparts.[87]

SEAL detachments in the U.S. Naval Reserve are manned exclusively with NSW veterans who have served at least 4 active years. Their principal purpose is to fill and augment the staffs of regular SEAL teams with individual ready reserves when required (Army and Air Force reserve component SOF, in contrast, are called up mainly as units).[88]

Waterborne Transportation. SEALs rely on various delivery vehicles to put them ashore at the right places and times, then rendezvous and recover. Fixed-wing aircraft, helicopters, submarines, and assorted surface craft all have distinctive advantages and disadvantages.

Infiltration/exfiltration by submarine, the most clandestine method, is feasible regardless of weather. Dry deck shelters, installed just before each mission and removed immediately thereafter, allow host ships to launch and recover SEAL delivery vehicles (SDV) while submerged. Capacities, however, are limited, because SDVs carry just two crew members and four combat swimmers with their cargo in fully flooded compartments.[89]

SEALs rely most often on waterborne surface craft in situations that call for sizable forces and fast reaction. A mix of coastal/interdiction and riverine patrol boats, mini-armored troop carriers (MATC), and combat rubber raiding craft (CRRC) with distinctively different characteristics afford flexibility. Threats, availability, endurance, draft, range, signatures, armament, seaworthiness, and carrying capacities influence the choice for any given mission. Compromise solutions are common. New Cyclone class patrol ships, for example, have great range and endurance and can survive 10-foot waves, but cannot move long distances fast enought for rapid response purposes. Rubber raiding craft can be air dropped but are unarmed and perform less well in rough water.[90]

SEAL platoons and supporting boat unit crews train together routinely throughout 18-month predeployment, deployment, and post-deployment cycles. They can thus capitalize on individual as well as collective strengths, and compensate for weaknesses.[91]

Collective Results. The Naval Special Warfare Command is stronger today than it was 6 six years ago, despite a shaky start.

Senior Navy officials, who fought unsuccessfully to retain control, at first treated NSW forces like unfaithful shipmates. Senior officials at USSOCOM, the gaining command, saw "reluctant dragons." Present relations, however, are almost ideal, according to the NAVSPECWARCOM Commander and his staff.[92] NSW forces, which specialize in littoral warfare, can help the conventional open ocean ("blue water") Navy make a smooth transition to "green" or "brown" water (close to coasts) in conformance with current doctrine.[93] Small NSW boats, which many Third World countries find less threatening to their sovereignty than big Navy ships, help DoD accomplish important peacetime missions. Programs completed and in progress give SEALs unprecedented worldwide capabilities. Promotion rates, retention rates, and morale are high.[94]

Marine Corps Contributions

Section 167, *Title 10, U.S. Code,* identifies SOF "as core forces or as augmenting forces in the Joint Chiefs of Staff Joint Strategic Capabilities Plan, Annex E" (dated 17 December 1985). The U.S. Marine Corps possesses no SOF on these terms, but selected Marine Expeditionary Units (MEU) since 1985 have been trained for and designated as "special operations capable" (SOC) prior to deployment.[95]

Each MEU is essentially a conventional task force with a reinforced infantry battalion, a reinforced helicopter squadron, and a service support group. Total personnel strength approximates 1,800 to 2,000. Assigned forces function together for a year, then return to parent organizations. Each MEU relies on a Navy Amphibious Ready Group (ARG) for mobility, sustainability, and communications/intelligence support. Such formations, forward deployed and fortuitously positioned, can sometimes help SOF infiltrate, exfiltrate, and otherwise perform important missions.[96]

One MEU (SOC) is always present in the Persian Gulf, another in the Mediterranean Sea. A third, shore-based on Okinawa, embarks when the Commander in Chief, U.S. Pacific Fleet, so directs. Close quarter battle, specialized demolition operations, clandestine reconnaissance and surveillance, tactical recovery of aircraft and personnel, *in extremis* hostage recovery, and the seizure or destruction of offshore oil production facilities receive attention during predeployment training. Each MEU must demonstrate required degrees of proficiency before it receives the (SOC) designation. USSOCOM and Marine Corps officials generally agree that no greater USMC contribution is necessary.[97]

USSOCOM and the Marine Corps have concluded a Memorandum of Agreement that established a USSOCOM/MC Board designed to "advise and make recommendations to USCINCSOC and the Commandant of the Marine Corps on policies, concepts, and issues which may be beneficial to both." The Board meets quarterly or on request. PSYOP and civil affairs support for MEU (SOC) and possible assignment of Army, Navy, and/or Air Force SOF officers to facilitate special operations training at Quantico, VA, Camp LeJeune, NC, and Camp Pendleton, CA, are typical topics for discussion.[98]

Joint Special Operations Command

The Joint Special Operations Command (JSOC) at Fort Bragg, NC, unlike USASOC, AFSOC, and NAVSPECWARCOM, is a multiservice component of USSOCOM. The prime directives of that headquarters are to study joint special operations requirements and techniques; ensure interoperability and equipment standardization; plan and conduct joint special operations exercises and training; develop joint SOF tactics; and provide the joint service expertise for a standing Joint Special Operations Task Force.[99]

Special Mission Units

An independent Special Operations Review Group, convened at JCS request after U.S. SOF failed to rescue hostages from Iran in April 1980, "recommended that a Counterterrorist Joint Task Force (CTJTF) be established as a field agency of the Joint Chiefs of Staff with permanently assigned staff personnel and certain assigned forces." The CTJTF, as directed by the National Command Authorities, "would plan, train for, and conduct operations to counter terrorist activities directed against U.S. interests, citizens, and/or property outside the United States." The group concluded that this activity would "provide the NCA with a range of options...from a small force of highly specialized personnel to a larger joint force. The Commander, CTJTF, would be responsible directly to the Joint Chiefs of Staff."[100]

A Standing Joint Special Operations Task Force, now part of

USSOCOM, has informally assumed direct action and strategic reconnaissance responsibilities, as well as counterterrorism. Its organization, strength, techniques, and activities generally are classified, but public statements and congressional testimony by General Stiner when he was CINCSOC identify the Army's Delta Force and SEAL Team 6 as permanently assigned Special Mission Units (SMUs).[101] Rangers and elements of the Special Operations Aviation Regiment (SOAR) augment as required. Selected Air Force crews routinely train with the SMUs.[102]

Delta Force assessment and selection procedures in some respects parallel those previously described for SEALs. Officers and noncommisioned officers (NCOs) receive identical treatment. All must be male, be at least 22 years of age, be airborne qualified or volunteer for airborne training, pass rigorous physical fitness tests and security investigations, and have no history of recurring disciplinary actions. Officers must be captains or majors, possess a college degree, be graduates of their basic branch advance course, and have at least 12 months of successful command experience. NCOs must have attained the rank of sergeant, have at least 4 years service, have attained a minimum GT score of 110 and a passing score in their primary specialty, and have 2 years active duty remaining.[103]

"We start out with an audience of 3,000," General Stiner explained. A preliminary screening leaves an average of 6 to 10 survivors and is followed by 6 months of four-phase intensified training. Stress tests and psychological evaluations separate unworthy applicants. Those who demonstrate superlative courage, self-discipline, intellect, and physical condition serve apprenticeships for 18 months with a Special Forces " 'A' detachment or a six-man shooter team in Delta or SEAL Team 6" before they are fully certified.[104]

Small teams, tailored for each task, count on speed, surprise, shock action, audacity, deception, and finely honed skills to accomplish surgical strikes against time-sensitive point targets despite adverse odds. A Ranger battalion, for example, might be the most appropriate instrument to seize and temporarily secure a particular piece of property, such as an airfield or a city block. Special Mission Units would be the most appropriate instrument to rescue hostages, retrieve valuable items, or disarm bombs inside a particular building on that property.[105] Prior planning (and rehearsals whenever practical) improve prospects for success. Alert forces on call "can be 'wheels up' in 4 hours with a requirement to go anywhere in the world," according to General Stiner.[106]

Margins for error are slim, and failure could discomfit the U.S. Government. USSOCOM consequently emphasizes programs and furnishes funds that maximize SMU capabilities and minimize limitations. CINCSOC considers the time, money, and attention expended to be cost effective, because enlisted members of Special Mission Units may remain as long as they are able to meet exacting standards.

Notes

1. *Memorandum for Mr. John Collins*, ASD SO/LIC, 12 July 1993, updated orally 13 July 1993.

2. *SO/LIC Accomplishments*, ASD SO/LIC memorandum, 29 June 1993, 1-3.

3. Ibid., 1, 4.

4. *OASD (SO/LIC) Research Program*, ASD SO/LIC, 21 May 1993.

5. *SO/LIC Accomplishments*, 3, 4.

6. *USSOCOM Command Intelligence Strategy Document*, April 1993, unclassified Executive Summary.

7. *Joint Pub 3-05: Doctrine for Joint Special Operations* (Washington, DC: Office of the Chairman of the Joint Chiefs of Staff, 1992), V 7-9; General Robert C. Kingston, U.S. Army (Ret.), *Intelligence for Low-Intensity Conflict: U.S. Problems and Options*, paper prepared for a General Accounting Office conference, Worldwide Threat, 30 October 1991; telephone conversation with Lieutenant General Samuel V. Wilson, USA (Ret.), 5 April 1993.

8. *Special Operations Intelligence*, a USSOCOM J-2 memorandum, 12 May 1993, 2, 4-5; *Deficiencies: Past-1987, FY 93-99*, a USSOCOM J-2 chart, April 1993.

9. See, for example, Stansfield Turner, "Intelligence for a New World Order," *Foreign Affairs* (Fall 1991): 153-159.

10. *Special Operations Intelligence*, 1-5; one-page USSOCOM memorandum, *USSOCOM Joint Intelligence Center*, 26 March 1993, *Intelligence Support to SOCs*, 28 April 1993, and *SOF Intelligence Systems*, 26 April 1993; *SOF Intel--Then/Now*, USSOCOM J-2 memorandum, 7 May 1993.

11. *SOF Intel--Then/Now*, 3.

12. Secretary of Defense, *Report on the Bottom Up Review* (Washington, DC: Office of the Secretary of Defense, 1993).

13. *The Planning Process of the USSOCOM Planning, Programming, and Budgeting System*, draft, May 1993.

14. Ibid., II-6, IV 2-6, D 2-3, and appendix C.

15. Ibid., II 3, 6-7, IV 5-6, and appendix D.

16. Ibid., II 5-6, IV 2; *USSOCOM Long Range Plan*, draft, undated (April 1993).

17. *Directive Nr. 70-2: Requirements System, Special Operations Peculiar Equipment*, USSOCOM, 24 June 1992.

18. *Active Component End Strength: Total Military and Civilian*, USSOCOM, 21 March 1993; *Resource Summary*, USSOCOM, 19 April 1993.

19. Roundtable discussions at USSOCOM and with component commands, 26-30 April 1993; Secretary of Defense, *Annual Report to the President and the Congress* (Washington, DC: GPO, 1993), 104-105.

20. *Directive Nr. 1-4: U.S. Special Operations Command Programming System*, 5 May 1993, 1, A-3.

21. Ibid., 2, A-1.

22. Comments on a draft of this report by the Director of Resources (J-8), USSOCOM. For descriptions of selected SOF programs in seven categories, see James R. Locher III and General Carl W. Stiner, *U.S. Special Operations Forces: Posture Statement* (Washington, DC: Assistant Secretary of Defense (SO/LIC), 1993), appendix A.

23. USSOCOM J-8 memorandum in response to author's written questions, untitled, undated.

24. Correspondence from USSOCOM's Washington Office, 18 May 1993.

25. Comments on a draft of this report by J-8, USSOCOM, 10 June 1993.

26. Locher and Stiner, 1992, C2 (updated informally in June 1993), and 1993, 28-30 and appendix C.

27. See, for example, David Morrell, *First Blood* (NY: Armchair Detective Library, 1972); Stein, Jeff, *A Murder in Wartime* (NY: St. Martin's Press, 1992).

28. General Carl W. Stiner, memorandum, *CINCSOC's FY 93 Priorities*, 22 October 1992, 1, 3; Lieutenant General Wayne A. Downing concurred in a related memorandum, same title, 13 November 1992.

29. *Collins "SOF Report" for Congress*, USSOCOM J-1 memorandum, 16 April 1993.

30. Marc Barnes, "Ex-Bragg Soldier Pleads Not Guilty to Rape Charges," *Fayetteville Observer-Times*, 27 April 1993, B1.

31. Quotation is contained in Bill Keller, "Special Forces are Termed Short of Aircraft," *New York Times*, 9 February 1986, 39; "Interview With Noel C. Koch," *Armed Forces Journal*, March 1985, 50.

32. Benjamin F. Schemmer, "December Was Not a Good Month for USAF Special Operations," *Armed Forces Journal*, January 1986, 26; Interview With Koch," 48.

33. Ross S. Kelly, "U.S. Special Operations: Doctrine Versus Hardware," *Defense & Foreign Affairs*, November 1984, 28-29.

34. Locher and Stiner, 1993, appendix A; Ken York, Glenn W. Goodman, Jr., et al., SOF "Special Report," *Armed Forces Journal*, November 1993, 28-39.

35. Stiner, *Priorities*, 1-2, 4.

36. Locher and Stiner, 1993, B-2, B-3, B-4; *Proposed Revisions to JCS Draft Roles and Missions Study*, USSOCOM memorandum, 5 January 1993, 4; correspondence from USSOCOM J-3, *Joint Special Operations School Integration Committee*, 25 May 1993.

37. For a review of regional idiosyncrasies that affect abilities to communicate effectively with foreigners, see James C. Boston, *An Address on Cross-Cultural Understanding*, delivered at the Industrial College of the Armed Forces, Washington, DC, 9 November 1966; input to this report by John Roberts, Betac Corporation, undated, 14-15.

38. Locher and Stiner, 1993, 15-26.

39. *Talking Paper on Special Operations Forces Support Activity (SOFSA)* and associated briefing slides, USSOCOM, undated; *USSOCOM Joint Operational Stocks (JOS) Program*, USSOCOM memorandum plus vugraphs, furnished to author, 29 April 1993.

40. *Talking Paper on Special Operations Force Support Activity*; response to author's written questions, USSOCOM J-4, undated.

41. *USSOCOM Joint Operational Stocks Program*, vugraphs furnished to author.

42. *Chronology*, provided by JFK Special Warfare Museum, Fort Bragg, NC, 26 May.

43. *Memorandum of Agreement Between U.S. Army and U.S. Special Operations Command*, signed 17 February 1993 and 28 January 1993.

44. *Chronology*, 3-4; Locher and Stiner, 1993, B-2.

45. Draft *DA Pamphlet 600-3*, (Special Printing): *Commissioned Officer Development and Career Management*, Washington, Hq. Dept. of the Army, 21 June 1991, chapter 14; *After Action Review—Special Forces Officer Branch Chief (14 June 90 - 30 June 92)* (Washington, DC: U.S. Total Army Personnel Command, 1992); roundtable discussion with Army SOF officers in the Pentagon, 20 April 1993; discussion with Lieutenant General Wayne A. Downing, April 1993.

46. *Chronology*, 3; telephone conversation with Special Forces staff officers, 27 May 1993.

47. *USASFC Commander's Readiness/Training Briefing to USSOCOM*, FY 1993, vugraphs furnished to author.

48. *Mission Statement*, a memorandum for Commander, U.S. Army Special Operations Integration Command (Airborne), from Commanding General USASOC, Fort Bragg, NC, 12 April 1993.

49. David W. Hogan, Jr., *Raiders or Elite Infantry? The Changing Role of the U.S. Army Rangers from Dieppe to Grenada* (Westport, CN: Greenwood Press, 1992).

50. *Ranger Regiment Commander's Readiness/Training Briefing to USSOCOM*, FY 1993, vugraphs furnished to author; Downing, 1993.

51. *SOAR Commander's Readiness/Training Briefing to CINCSOC*, FY 1993; Downing, 1993.

52. *Chronology*, 3; *Designation of Psychological Operations and Civil Affairs as Special Operations Forces*, Memorandum from Secretary of Defense to Secretaries of the Military Departments and the Chairman of the Joint Chiefs of Staff, 3 March 1993.

53. *Civil Affairs*, 6 USASOC vugraphs furnished to author; Downing, 1993; *Conduct of the Persian Gulf War*, Final Report to Congress (Washington, DC: Dept. of Defense, 1992), J-23 to J-26. For typical CA tasks, see Lt. Col. Walter E. Wright and Maj. Ronald L. Fiegle, "Civil Affairs Support in Operations Other than War," *Military Review*, October 1993, 27-33; also, *Civil Affairs Implications for Future Contingencies*, prepared by a 352d CA Command reservist during active duty training with USCENTCOM J-5, 1993.

54. *Persian Gulf War*, J-20 to J-23; *Leaflets of the Persian Gulf War*, Fort Bragg, NC, 4th PSYOP Group, undated; Downing, 1993.

55. Alfred H. Paddock, Jr., *U.S. Army Special Warfare: Its Origins* (Washington, DC: National Defense University Press, 1982), 1; *USAJFKSWCS Commander's Readiness/Training Briefing to USSOCOM*, FY 1993, vugraphs furnished to author.

56. *Chronology*, 3, 4; *Special Operations Coordination Element SOCOORD and Special Operations Command & Control Element SOCCE*, USASOC, 1989 to 1992, vugraphs furnished to author.

57. "The Special Operations Schoolhouse," *Army*, April 1992, 40-42; *USAJFKSWCS Commander's Readiness/Training Briefing to USSOCOM*.

58. *Chronology*, 3; telephone conversation with Army staff officers, 28 May 1993.

59. *USAJFKSWCS Commander's Readiness/Training Briefing to USSOCOM*, vugraphs furnished to author.

60. Major General Hugh L. Cox III, former Deputy Commander in Chief of USSOCOM, "The 1980's: A Decade of Evolution for Air Force Special Operations," *Air Commando Newsletter*, December 1992, 11, 21, 24. See also Major John A. Hill, *Air Force Special Operations Forces*, Research Report No. AU-ARO-92-3 (Maxwell AFB, AL: Air University Press), 1-3; *Chronology of the Twenty-Third Air Force/Air Force Special Operations Command 1983-1992* (Hurlburt Field, FL: AFSOC Historian) 1-17.

61. *AFSOC Emerging Doctrine*, vugraphs furnished to author, undated; Hill, 4-16.

62. Twenty-Third Air Force, 9-17, passim; Cox, 24-26.

63. *Memorandum of Agreement Between U.S. Air Force and U.S. Special Operations Command*, signed 5 August and 16 September 1989.

64. US Air Force Fact Sheets, January 1993: *Air Force Special Operations Command*; *1st Special Operations Wing*; *720th Special Tactics* Group; *352d Special Operations Group*; and *353d Special Operations Group*; USAF Fact Sheets, March 1993: *U.S. Air Force Special Operations School* and *Special Missions Operational Test and Evaluation Center*. For a detailed discussion of Special Tactics teams, see Frank Oliveri, "When the LZ is Hot," *Air Force Magazine*, February 1994, 29-34.

65. James C. Hyde, "Air Force Special Operations Command Can't Shake Those Growing Pains," *Armed Forces Journal*, May 1993, 45; Benjamin F. Schemmer, "Four New SOF Aircraft Are Late and Way Over Cost, but...," *Armed Forces Journal*, July 1991, 42-43.

66. *Cost Accounting Data for SOF Airlift*, memorandum from Deputy Secretary of Defense for Secretary of the Army and Secretary of the Air Force, 31 October 1986, and *AFSOC: America's Specialized Air Power, A Step Ahead in a Changing World*, April 1993, vugraph furnished to author,

67. US Air Force Fact Sheet, February 1993, *MC-130 E/H Combat Talon I/II*; *Program Status Briefings*, AFSOC Acquisition Management Division, April 1993; *Combat Talon Employment Mission Data (Talon I)*, FAX from Hq USAF (XOFU), 9 March 1993.

68. US Air Force Fact Sheet, February 1993, *AC-130 A/H Spectre Gunship*; *Program Status Briefings*, updated by AFSOC Acquisition Management Division, 2 June 1993.

69. US Air Force Fact Sheet, February 1993, *HC-130N/P Combat Shadow*; telephone conversation with Lieutenant Colonel Bernie Moore, Hq USAF (AF/XOXS), 2 June 1993.

70. US Air Force Fact Sheet, February 1993, *EC-130E Commando Solo*; EC-130 E Command Solo and Senior Hunter vugraph, *AFSOC: America's Specialized Air Power*, furnished to author.

71. US Air Force Fact Sheet, February 1993, *MH-53J Pave Low III*, amplified by AFSOC Acquisition Management Division, 3 June 1993.

72. US Air Force Fact Sheet, February 1993, *MH-60G Pave Hawk*, *AFSOC Program Status Briefings*.

73. US Air Force Fact Sheet, March 1992, *Special Missions Operational Test and Evaluation Center*; written comments on a draft of this report, USSOCOM Washington Office, 10 June 1993.

74. Schemmer, *Not a Good Month*, 26.

75. Point paper, *AFSOC Readiness Since 1980*, 18 June 1993.

76. *Strategic Plan* (Hurlburt Field, FL: AFSOC Public Affairs, 1993), 16-17, 20-21.

77. Roundtable discussions at AFSOC, 27 April 1993; Hyde, 45; US Air Force Fact Sheet, January 1993, *720th Special Tactics Group*.

78. Five AFSOC vugraphs, April 1993, furnished to author.

79. U.S. Air Force Fact Sheet, March 1993, *U.S. Air Force Special Operations School*; "Air Force Special Operations School: An Emphasis on Education," *Special Warfare*, May 1993, 10-13.

80. *NAVSPECWARCOM Command History*, 1987, 1; 1988, 2; and 1991, 2.

81. "Naval Special Warfare," *NAVSPECWARCOM Fact File*, January 1993, 1-2; *What Is Naval Special Warfare?* NAVSPECWARCOM, undated, 14A; roundtable discussion at NAVSPECWARCOM, 30 April 1993.

82. *NAVSPECWARCOM Command History*, 1988, 2,3; "Naval Special Warfare Command," 1; memorandum for the Secretary of Defense through the Under Secretary of Defense for Policy from the Assistant Secretary of Defense (International Security Affairs), *Assignment of Naval Special Warfare (NSW) Groups to USSOCOM*, 9 October 1987; two memoranda from Secretary of Defense Weinberger to Chairman of the Joint Chiefs of Staff and to Secretary of the Navy, *Assignment of Naval Special Warfare (NSW) Groups to CINCSOC*, 23 October 1987.

83. "Naval Special Warfare Command; *NAVSPECWARCOM Command History*, 1989, vi.

84. Comments on a draft of this report by ASD SO/LIC, 1 July 1993; *NAVSPECWARCOM Command History*, 1988, 2,3; *Memorandum of Agreement Between U.S. Navy and U.S. Special Operations Command*, signed 8 August and 28 August 1992.

85. "Sea, Air, Land (SEAL) Teams," "Naval Special Warfare," "Weapons," "Desert Patrol Vehicle (DPV)," and "Scuba," all in *NAVSPECWARCOM Fact File*; Greg Walker, "Elite SEAL Units", *Combat Arms*, November 1989, 26-32; Antonio Scialdone, "Naval Special Operations: A Future?", *Military Technology*, April 1984, 80-82, 84-85,

88, 89.

86. "Basic Underwater Demotion/SEAL (BUD/S) Training," *NAVSPECWARCOM Fact File*; "Naval Special Warfare Center: 'Schoolhouse' for Naval Special Operations," *Special Warfare*, May 1993, 4-17.

87. *What Is Naval Special Warfare?*, 9-10; "Schoolhouse' for Naval Special Operations," 17; roundtable discussion at NAVSPECWARCOM, 30 April 1993; *NSW Training Cycle*, 4 NAVSPECWARCOM vugraphs, undated, furnished to author.

88. Roundtable discussion with Navy SOF in the Pentagon, 23 April 1993.

89. *What Is Naval Special Warfare?*, 7A; "SEAL Delivery Vehicle (SDV) MK VIII" and "Dry Deck Shelter (DDS)," *NAVSPECWARCOM Fact File*.

90. *What is Naval Special Warfare?*, 8, 11, 25-28, 30-37; Special Boat Section, *NAVSPECWARCOM Fact File*.

91. *What Is Naval Special Warfare?*, 13-14.

92. Roundtable discussion at NAVSPECWARCOM, 30 April 1993.

93. Basic elements of post-Cold War naval doctrine are described in *From the Sea: Preparing the Naval Service for the 21st Century*, a Navy and Marine Corps White Paper (Washington, DC: Dept. of the Navy, 1992).

94. Roundtable discussion at NAVSPECWARCOM, 30 April 1993; *What Is Naval Special Warfare?*, 44-49.

95. For background and early development, see Bemjamin F. Schemmer, "Commandant Directs Marines to Sharpen Their Inherent Special Ops Capability," *Armed Forces Journal*, October 1985, 24-25; Harry M. Murdock, "MAU (SOC): A Powerful Maritime Force," *Marine Corps Gazette*, August 1987, 67-70.

96. . . . *From the Sea: Naval Expeditionary Forces Shaped for Joint Operations*, 7 vugraphs, furnished to author;discussion with members of SO/LIC Branch, HQ USMC, 2 June 1993.

97. Ibid; written comments on a draft of this report by SO/LIC Branch, HQ USMC, 8 June 1993.

98. *Memorandum of Agreement Between U.S. Special Operations Command (USSOCOM) and the U.S. Marine Corps, Subject: USSOCOM - Marine Corps (SOCOM-MC) Board*, 1 April 1993.

99. Locher and Stiner, 1993, B-5.

100. *Rescue Mission Report* (the Holloway Report) (Washington, DC: Joint Chiefs of Staff Special Operations Review Group, 1980), 61, 63.

101. Congress, House, *Department of Defense Appropriations for 1992*, part 2, Special Operations Command, Hearings Before a Subcommittee of the Committee on Appropriations, 102d Cong., 2d sess., 1991, 189-256.

102. Congress, House, *Department of Defense Appropriations for 1987*, part 1, Secretary and Chief of Staff of the Army, Hearings Before a Subcommittee of the Committee on Appropriations, 99th Cong., 2d sess., 1986, 139.

103. "Delta Seeks Recruits," *Special Warfare*, January 1994, 51.

104. Congress, House, *Department of Defense Appropriations for 1992*, 228; Charlie A. Beckwith, *Military Special Operations*, presentation to Betac Corporation, 16 January 1987, section VII and enclosure 3. For some insights into SEAL Team 6 training, see Richard Marcinko, *Rogue Warrior* (NY: Pocket Books, 1992), 227-257.

105. For six typical missions that SMUs might perform, see Leroy Thompson, *The Rescuers: The World's Top Anti-Terrorist Units* (Boulder, CO: Paladin Press, 1986), 19-54.

106. Presentation by General Stiner at the Fourth Annual SO/LIC Symposium hosted by the American Defense Preparedness Association, 8 December 1992; *Characteristics of Special Operations*, 6 unclassified vugraphs furnished to author by Joint Special Operations Command, undated.

V. Theater Special Operations Commands

U.S. Special Operations Command organizes, equips, trains, and provides Army, Navy, and Air Force SOF for use by five regionally oriented U.S. unified commands. Each regional CINC delegates operational control to a theater special operations command (SOC). The Commander of U.S. Forces Korea has also established a SOC for such purposes.

Common Characteristics

All six SOCs share some important characteristics that strongly influence capabilities, limitations, and methods of operation. All express similar opinions concerning relationships with USSOCOM:

- Every theater had some sort of special operations command before Congress enacted the first SO/LIC legislation in 1986. SOCs supporting U.S. European, Pacific, Central, and Southern Commands became multiservice subordinate unified commands with broad, continuing missions in 1985-86, while the SOC supporting Atlantic Command followed suit in 1987. The SOC in Korea, which is a standing joint task force, performs similar functions.[1] All six organizations provide a focal point for in-theater SOF, form nuclei for Joint Special Operations Task Forces (JSOTF), and furnish the expertise needed to employ SOF effectively in concert with conventional forces or independently.[2]

- Foreign internal defense (FID) is the predominant peacetime mission everywhere except Korea.

Counternarcotics operations are an important aspect of FID, particularly in SOUTHCOM, and humanitarian assistance receives greater attention than in the past. Ultimate aims are to reduce regional instability, prevent violence, strengthen U.S. alliances, and encourage democratic systems of government that respect human rights. Top priority missions connected with crises and other contingencies include direct action and counterterrorism. Special reconnaissance contributes to the successful accomplishment of all SOF missions.[3]

- Regionally oriented U.S. unified commands and their SOCs all rely essentially on the same sources of special operations doctrine and policy. Annex E to the Joint Strategic Capabilities Plan (JSCP) describes SOF missions, apportions SOF to theater CINCs, and disseminates basic policy guidance. The *Joint Pub 3-05* series, still evolving, dispenses fundamental doctrine.[4] Documents developed by USSOCOM and its component commands elaborate and expound on additional subjects.[5] Each CINC promulgates policies specifically for his Area of Responsibility (AOR). A small special operations staff section helps plan and supervise all in-theater SOF activities, acts as a conduit to and from the SOC, sometimes manages sensitive, compartmented ("black") programs, and otherwise assists.[6]

- Each theater special operations command is spartanly staffed. A comprehensive manpower requirements survey conducted in 1992 recommended that total peacetime authorizations increase from 192 to 369. The Joint Staff, however, imposed a 20 percent decrement on all headquarters staffs, reducing manning levels to 295. Wartime manning reflected on table 3 probably will increase after an ongoing review is complete.[7]

- Every SOC requires augmentation to cope with sizable crises and other contingencies. Reserve Component individual mobilization augmentees train with them annually, but reinforcement procedures presently are *ad hoc*. No formal agreements as yet prescribe what packets USSOCOM or the services are prepared to provide any SOC. The USSOCOM J-5, however, is developing a "battle roster" of active duty SOF staff officers to assist theater special operations commands during selected major

Table 3. *Theater SOC headquarters manning*

	Peacetime			Wartime
	FY 1992 baseline	Assigned mid-1993	Proposed strength	Proposed strength
SOCLANT	17	20	33	85
SOCCENT	31	38	69	140
SOCEUR	58	59	83	150
SOCSOUTH	31	39	71	140
SOCPAC	43	44	88	150
SOC-K	12	9	25	97
	192	209	369	762

exercises and otherwise augment wherever needed on short notice. Complete staff and equipment packages also are in preparation.[8]

- Only SOCEUR possesses dedicated communications. Its 42-man detachment, however, is scheduled for inactivation unless manpower spaces are restored. SOCLANT and SOCSOUTH rely mainly on augmentation from USASOC's 112th Signal Battalion at Fort Bragg, NC, which employs outdated equipment (analog instead of digital switching, for example). SOCCENT depends almost exclusively on the Joint Communications Support Element (JCSE), which the Chairman of the Joint Chiefs of Staff tasks to serve wherever and whenever serious shortfalls develop. SOCPAC and SOC-K rely on *ad hoc* arrangements. CINCs and SOC commanders consequently feel vulnerable, because their abilities to provide responsive, reliable, interoperative communications in the clutch are uncertain and constrained.[9]

- All theater CINCs and SOCs increasingly incorporate psychological operations and civil affairs into plans, training, and operations.[10] All express concern that most CA units reside in Reserve Components, which are more difficult to reach than counterparts in the active U.S. Army. Needs for reserve PSYOP forces are much less; only 108 were called to active duty during *Desert Storm.*[11]

- Relationships between theater CINCs and the Special Mission Units (SMUs) once were strained, partly because SMU teams respond to U.S. National Command Authorities rather than regional Commanders in Chief. Interactions with EUCOM, LANTCOM, PACOM, CENTCOM, and SOUTHCOM remain excellent, despite some reported disagreements about control during unsuccessful attempts to apprehend Somali warlord Mohammed Farah Aideed in autumn 1993. SOCLANT and SOC-Korea seldom interact with SMUs.[12]

- Assessments of USSOCOM during the course of this study were universally positive. As CINCs and theater SOC commanders see it, the absence of a four-star SOF proponent before 1987 precluded the development of a cohesive military special operations community. They appreciate the professional advice, special funding, and logistic support that USSOCOM now provides. They strongly approve "one-stop shopping" currently available for superlatively trained Special Operations Forces and find that direct liaison authority between theater SOCs and USSOCOM's subordinate commands is the best way to ensure that CINC requirements are met as expeditiously as possible.[13]

Unique Characteristics

All six regionally oriented special operations commands exhibit unique characteristics. Perceived threats, geographic circumstances, types of contingencies, the intensity of crises, and other factors vary (see figure 5 for respective Areas of Responsibility).

SOCLANT

Atlantic Command's immense Area of Responsibility (AOR) is mainly water; 39 islands comprise the only land.[14] Greenland, by far the largest, has a population half that of Peoria, IL. The most densely settled islands are small, except for Cuba, Hispaniola (Haiti and Dominican Republic), Jamaica, and Puerto Rico, all in the Caribbean Basin.

Figure 5. U.S. Unified Commands:
Areas of Responsibility

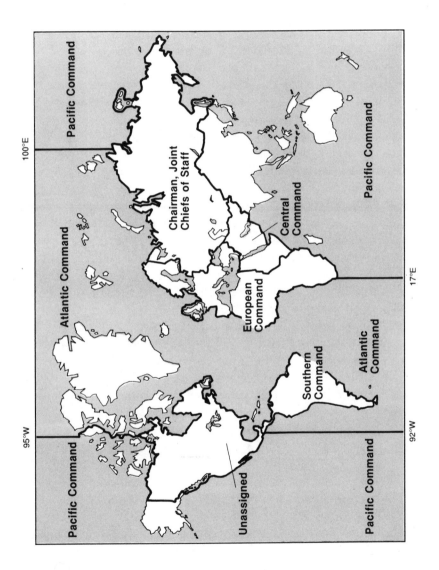

CINCLANT and staff, located in Norfolk, VA, seldom expressed interest in special operations throughout the Cold War, when conventional naval matters took precedence. Special Operations Command, Atlantic (SOCLANT) is the smallest of five SOCs designated as subordinate U.S. unified commands. It is the only one not authorized a brigadier general. Other officers assigned "are totally dedicated, hard-working, and professional," but are not competitive with peers in their parent services, according to SOCLANT's Commander. The percentage of those passed over for promotion or selected for early retirement is well above average. No SOF are permanently assigned or forward based, except one Naval Special Warfare Unit. The LANTCOM staff retains responsibility for counterterrorism, counternarcotics, psychological operations, civil affairs, and compartmented "black" programs.[15]

The pattern just depicted is starting to change. Admiral Paul David Miller, the present CINCLANT, expresses a personal interest in SOF. Vigorous training programs that emphasize joint operations focus increasingly on such missions as peace promoting, peacekeeping, peace enforcement, coalition building, nation assistance, disaster relief, domestic support, and humanitarian assistance, all of which are long-standing SOF specialties. Admiral Miller, who recently received a change in his charter that gave LANTCOM jurisdiction over most conventional forces in the Continental United States,[16] wants to weld conventional and SOF capabilities within Adaptive Joint Force Packages. He is working closely with CINCSOC to achieve that objective.[17]

Whereas SOCLANT until recently rarely ventured far from home station (most training took place at Fort Story, VA), Deployment for Training programs now occur routinely in or near the Caribbean. Ten countries participated during FY 1993, and an even dozen during FY 1994. Military Information Support teams (MIST) conduct overt peacetime psychological operations that support humanitarian/civic action/counternarcotics activities and otherwise help SOF accomplish assigned missions.[18]

SOCLANT's operating tempo remains moderate. Civil affairs and PSYOP help for Haitian refugees at Guantanamo Naval Base have been the main exception. The pace, however, could quickly pick up if internal disturbances cause Cuba and/or Haiti in particular to demand greater attention by U.S. SOF.[19]

SOCCENT

Central Command's Area of Responsibility contains 18 countries in Northeast Africa and Southwest Asia, plus Afghanistan and Pakistan (figure 5). CENTCOM headquarters, collocated with USSOCOM at MacDill AFB, FL, is seven time zones removed as a minimum; the farthest reaches are nine zones away. The region is politically, ethnically, and culturally complex, and diversified populations speak many languages, of which various Arabic dialects, Farsi, Urdu, Pashtu, Dari, Amharic, Somali, and Swahili are most prevalent.

No Special Operations Forces are permanently stationed in CENTCOM's AOR. USSOCOM and its component commands provide SOF from a pool that contains Army Special Forces, Rangers, Naval Special Warfare Units, fixed- and rotary-wing aircraft, PSYOP, and Civil Affairs. Special Mission Units participate whenever appropriate. An Amphibious Ready Group that includes a Marine Expeditionary Unit (Special Operations Capable), SEALs, and aviation assets normally is present within the AOR. That mix is adequate, according to the SOCCENT Commander, although CA/PSYOP support depends heavily on selective personnel call-ups from Reserve Components .[20]

Potential augmentation requirements range from a 12-man Special Forces A team or a flight of Spectre gunships to reinforcements on the scale of those during *Desert Storm*, which employed more than 9,000 SOF under SOCCENT control (the SOC Commander at that time was an Army colonel; a brigadier general has filled that slot since January 1993). Forces that USSOCOM provides as a rule "are highly skilled, superbly trained, and are cohesive professional units."[21]

The polyglot complexion of CENTCOM's AOR exacerbates foreign language problems. The supply of skilled linguists has increased but remains insufficient; PSYOP and civil affairs specialists in the active U.S. Army seldom attend language school because commitments are ceaseless and their numbers are few. Less than a handful of SOF linguists, for example, are fluent in Iraqi dialects. Only one man spoke Somali when Operation *Restore Hope* erupted in December 1992. CENTCOM consequently had to hire locals who could converse in English, an undesirable but unavoidable expedient. Warlord Aideed's son, a U.S. Marine corporal, served as a translator until his presence was deemed impolitic.[22]

SOCCENT currently exercises in several Arab States, Pakistan,

Somalia, Kenya, and Ethiopia. A Military Training Team is scheduled for Ethiopia. Ongoing efforts seek an entré in Eritrea. The fast tempo that started with Operation *Desert Shield* in August 1990 continues. Quick response actions have been common. SOCCENT, for example, deployed as a Joint Special Operations Task Force (JSOTF) to punish warlord Aideed for attacking UN peacekeepers in Mogadishu. The warning order came at 1100 hours on Sunday 6 June 1993; SOCCENT identified augmentation requirements before midnight; USSOCOM and CENTCOM provided forces on Monday; those forces departed for Mogadishu on Tuesday, arrived on Wednesday, and went into combat the following day. (Rangers and SMUs, who suffered 18 dead and 73 wounded during the worst shootout on 3 October 1993, were not under SOCCENT control.)[23]

Resultant strains are taking a toll. The Deputy Commander in Chief of Central Command, the CENTCOM staff, and SOCCENT officers all use the words "burn out." Allied schedules cause the small SOCCENT staff to burn midnight oil 7 days a week (people in Moslem countries, for example, do not work on Thursday or Friday). The time differential between Florida and the Middle East is 7 hours; consequently, jet lag from repetitious round trips is common. Operational taskings require SOC personnel to deploy often, sometimes for long periods (e.g., one sergeant was absent from MacDill AFB 32 out of 39 months after being assigned).[24]

SOCEUR

U.S. European Command is a well-developed theater that enjoyed top priority throughout Cold War confrontations between NATO and the Warsaw Pact. Special Operations Command, Europe (SOCEUR), located in Vaihingen, Germany, can trace its antecedents to World War II. The Area of Responsibility, which reaches from Norway's North Cape to the Cape of Good Hope, contains several trouble spots and potential flash points, of which Bosnia-Hercegovina, Libya, Liberia, Israel, and South Africa are among the most prominent (figure 5). Refugees from former Yugoslavia, right wing nationalists in Germany, unrest in Russia and neighboring states, and transnational terrorism cause security concerns in Western Europe.[25]

Forward-based Special Operations Forces under SOCEUR's control include one Army Special Forces battalion in Germany, a

Naval Special Warfare Unit in Scotland, and an Air Force special operations group in England. The latter contains three aircraft squadrons (MC-130 Combat Talons, MH-53J Pave Low helicopters, HC-130 Combat Shadows) and a Special Tactics Squadron. An active duty Civil Affairs company and a reserve CA Command periodically augment CINCEUR's staff; active and reserve component PSYOP units also assist. Their input is "particularly critical since only the United States has a fully functional military Psychological Operations system to support U.S., NATO, or UN operations in the USEUCOM AOR."[26]

SOCEUR's training program consists of "a combination of JCS exercises, unit funded Joint Combined Exchange Training (JCET) exercises with other nations, [and] seminar wargame events usually hosted by SOCEUR.... The 'program' is adequate, but funds, intratheater airlift and troop availability are not adequate."[27] Operations since *Desert Shield* started have absorbed additional time and personnel, typified by *Sharp Edge* (noncombatant evacuation from Liberia in 1990), *Provide Comfort* (humanitarian assistance to destitute Kurds in 1991), *Provide Hope* (aid to the Commonwealth of Independent States in 1991), and *Provide Promise* (primarily airdropped supplies for beleaguered Bosnians in 1993). [28]

All in-theater SOF were "operationally employed or on an operational alert status" as of June 10, 1993. Commitments "continue to impact SOF training...and adversely impact the quality of life for SOF personnel (primarily the 352d Special Operations Group)," according to the SOCEUR Commander. He has requested the following permanent reinforcements: a company of MH-60 Black Hawk helicopters, a SEAL platoon, a Naval Special Warfare Unit, a special operations support company, and part of a signal company. He deems the latter requirement particularly critical, because the pending deactivation of the 42-man SOCEUR Signal Detachment "will cripple" command/control and crisis response capabilities in his judgment.[29]

SOCEUR Headquarters also is shorthanded, because it serves Allied Command Europe (ACE), exercises operational control over in-theater SOF as a sub-unified command, and additionally is European Command's Special Operations staff directorate (ECSO). There is no J-3 Special Operations Division. No other SOC has three such responsibilities. Those relationships ensure that SOF are duly considered in plans but, because of limited manpower, "when

SOCEUR deploys for a major contingency operation only minimal ECSO functions are performed." Opportunities for error then increase.[30]

SOCSOUTH

Southern Command's Area of Responsibility includes 20 countries in Central and South America from Mexico's border with Guatemala and Belize to Cape Horn (figure 5). Each nation has distinctive characteristics, but the huge AOR nevertheless is fairly homogeneous despite great geographic differences (flatlands and mountain chains, jungles, swamps, and arable plains). Spanish is the prevalent language, except for Portuguese in Brazil. Lengthy rule by Iberian colonials left common cultures and institutions as a legacy. Distrust of "Yanqui imperialism," now muted but nevertheless notable, left common concerns for national sovereignty that restrict U.S. military activities.

Special Operations Command, South (SOCSOUTH), headquartered at Albrook Air Force Station, Panama, controls one Army Special Forces company, an Army special operations aviation detachment with MH-60 Black Hawks, and a Special Operations Support Command. U.S. Atlantic Fleet Detachment South controls a Naval Special Warfare Unit and a Special Boat Unit based at Rodman, Panama. Both support SOCSOUTH when CINCSOUTH so directs. Those forces, augmented by USSOCOM when required, regularly participate in small exercises with SOUTHCOM's 193d Infantry Brigade to ensure smooth interoperability. "Insufficient rotary-wing SOF aircraft and corresponding funding for flying hours," however, are significant constraints. "The use of conventional theater based aviation assets to support SOF [consequently] is being tested."[31]

"The political climate throughout Latin America does not easily allow for large scale exercises to be planned for or executed." SOCSOUTH seeks to compensate by using the Joint Readiness Training Center (JRTC) located at Fort Polk, Louisiana, but so doing degrades effectiveness compared with in-theater training.[32]

Central America was SOUTHCOM's center of attention until the 1990s, with particular concern for Nicaragua, El Salvador, and Panama. The current focus concentrates on countries that produce, and from which cartels export, illicit narcotics, particularly Colombia, Bolivia, and Peru. SOCSOUTH is an important player in efforts to discourage, disrupt, and interdict the production and dissemination of such drugs. Its principal programs emphasize advice and training designed to help host government forces attack sources and transportation systems most effectively.[33]

Terrorism is a favored tool of large drug cartels, which have more firepower and funds at their disposal than many national governments. The leader of one such conglomeration, for example, offered to "rent" the Bolivian Army for a week so he could defeat competitors. SOCSOUTH trains local anti-counterterrorism forces. U.S. Special Mission Units designed expressly to deal directly with terrorist incidents "exercise and train extensively in SOUTHCOM." Relationships among those elite groups, SOCSOUTH, and the theater CINC's *in extremis* force (CIF) are strong. Standard operating procedures for communications and control "have been proven repeatedly."[34]

SOCPAC

Pacific Command's watery domain is three time as large as LANTCOM's. Its Area of Responsibility also embraces a big chunk of Asian land mass, the continent of Australia, Madagascar, New Zealand, the Indonesian archipelago, Papua New Guinea, the Philippines, Japan, numerous small islands, and a total population that approximates 2.5 billion (figure 5). More than 30 million people speak one of 18 main languages; Burmese, Cambodian, and innumerable dialects add to this number. Consequently, strict priorities based on the best possible requirement forecasts are essential, because USSOCOM cannot produce enough culturally-attuned, language-qualified SOF for every district.

Special Operations Command, Pacific (SOCPAC), located at Camp H.M. Smith on Oahu, is as far from India, Burma, and Thailand as SOCCENT Headquarters is from the Middle East. SOF assigned to cover its extensive and complex AOR include an Army Special Forces battalion on Okinawa, a SEAL platoon collocated with a Naval Special Warfare Unit on Guam, and an Air Force special operations group that consists of three squadrons (MC-130 Combat Talons and HC-130 Combat Shadows at Kadena AB, Japan; MH-53J Pave Low helicopters at Osan, Korea). A Special Operations Support Command completes the in-theater complement. One Civil Affairs brigade in the Army Reserve prepares to assist.[35]

SOCPAC "relies heavily" on backup SOF in the Continental United States "to man its Joint Special Operations Task Force (JSOTF) headquarters and liaison positions, along with fillers for SOCPAC headquarters during exercises and contingencies." More would be needed to handle major emergencies. Travel times, however, are long and costs are high. Army Special Forces, Civil Affairs, and PSYOP units based at Fort Bragg, NC, for example, must cross 13 time zones to reach Thailand after stopping for instructions in Hawaii. AC-130 gunships seldom exercise in PACOM AOR. Active-duty reinforcements, who lack familiarity with allied and PACOM operating procedures, "usually have trouble getting up to speed quickly." Reserve Component SOF require extra training. Augmentees seldom come from the same source, so a break-in period almost always must precede employment. The SOCPAC Commander nevertheless believes that present arrangements are generally "adequate...to meet most USPACOM contingencies," even though the operational tempo "is often high, with SOF on-the-road, away from garrison locations, for long periods."[36]

SOCPAC headquarters and SOF are "fully integrated into the USCINCPAC Exercise Program." Its JSOTF, when formed, "is on the same organizational level as other components." Training areas on Okinawa and Guam are insufficient but, in compensation, SOCPAC annually conducts more than 30 smaller Foreign Internal Defense (FID) exercises in various countries, each "fully coordinated/approved/directed through the Joint/Combined Exchange Training (JCET) program....Host nation support is excellent." The number of fixed-wing SOF aircraft is "adequate" for such purposes, "but with only 4 MH-53s [Pave Low helicopters] available in theater, there is seldom enough vertical lift." That squadron based in Korea, moreover, "has been unable to get the JP-5 [aviation fuel] required to conduct deck landing qualifications on U.S. Navy ships."[37]

SOC-KOREA

Korea is the only theater within which U.S. and allied SOF are institutionally integrated. Special Operations Command, Korea (SOC-K), located in Seoul, is a standing joint task force controlled by the Commander, U.S. Forces Korea. It serves the Republic of Korea (ROK)/U.S. Combined Forces Command, is a component of the Combined Unconventional Warfare Task Force, and works closely with the ROK Army Special Warfare Command. Special operations accordingly are "thoroughly imbedded in operational plans."[38]

Tensions in Korea have remained high since 1953. SOC-K thus confronts a known enemy every day. Nevertheless, budgetary constraints compel its headquarters to operate on a shoestring. "SOC-K has no organic capability to communicate with higher, lower, or adjacent units..., has no intelligence collection, analysis, production, or dissemination capability, nor any targeting capability.... The only intelligence system available is a Korean Intelligence Support System (KISS) with no dedicated operator." Perhaps even more importantly, SOC-K relies on Reserve Components for 90 percent of the personnel it reportedly needs "to go to war." The essential lifesaver, as the SOC-K Commander sees it, "is a battle roster of active duty [USSOCOM] staff officers to reinforce SOC-K should hostilities commence." It is his opinion that "without this initiative, we would fail since our reserve augmentation staff wouldn't arrive in time nor be competent to function immediately in the high intensity battlefield confronting us in a Korean conflict."[39]

The Republic of Korea furnishes most SOF in theater. The fact that SOC-K controls just one Army Special Forces Detachment, therefore, lacks much significance, but the Pacific-wide shortage of U.S. special operations air power remains a pressing concern, "because the ROKs don't have a SOF air capability." The SOC-K Commander suggests that more is required "to maximize the huge ROK contribution."[40]

"On outbreak of hostilities, SOC-K combines with the Republic of Korea Special Warfare Command to form the Combined Unconventional Warfare Task Force (CUWTF)." The CUWTF concept is exercised three times yearly, but "full-up" augmentation for SOC-K has never occurred. "Therefore, while these 'canned' scenario exercises are considered successful, the actual wartime requirements" are still uncertain.[41]

Notes

1.   Messages from JCS authorizing the establishment of special operations commands as subordinate unified commands: to USCINCCENT, 5 February 1986, and to USCINCEUR and CINCSOUTH, 30 May 1986; JCS memorandums for USCINCPAC, undated (November 1986) and USCINCLANT, February 18, 1987; JCS

message to COMUSKOREA, 29 April 1988.

2. James R. Locher III and General Carl W. Stiner, *United States Special Operations Forces: Posture Statement*, (Washington, DC: Assistant Secretary of Defense [SO/LIC], 1993), B5.

3. Response by all regional CINCs/SOCs to the question, "Which of the nine specific SOF missions in *Title 10, USC*, are most important to your command?"

4. The foundation document is *Joint Pub 3-05: Doctrine for Joint Special Operations* (Washington, DC: Office of the Chairman, Joint Chiefs of Staff, 1992). See also *Joint Pub 3-05.3: Joint Special Operations Operational Procedures*, final draft, July 1993, and *Joint Pub 3-05.5: Joint Special Operations Targeting and Mission Planning Procedures*, final draft, July 1993.

5. A typical example is *AFSOC Emerging Doctrine*, 36 vugraphs furnished to author (Hurlburt Field, FL: AFSOC Hq, undated). Further discussion of one aspect is found in Major John A. Hill, "Command and Control of Air Force Special Operations Forces," in *AFSOC: A Unique Application of Aerospace Power* (Maxwell AFB, AL: Air University Press, 1993), 19-41.

6. Response by all regional CINCs/SOCs to the questions, "Who provides SOF policy guidance to your command? Is it adequate?" and "Does the CINC's staff have a J-3 SOD? If so, what functions does it perform?"

7. *Theater Special Operations Commands: A Manpower Study of the Special Operations Commands of the Five Unified Combatant Theater Commands* (Washington, DC: U.S. Army Force Integration Support Agency (USAFISA), 1992); response by all regional CINCs/SOCs to the questions, "Is your SOC adequately staffed?" and "What arrangements exist for USSOCOM to provide SOC augmentation packets in emergency?"

8. Ibid.; comments on a draft of this report by J-3 (SOD), 2 July 1993, 9.

9. Response by all regional CINCs/SOCs to the question, "What quantitative/qualitative deficiencies exist in SOC personnel and/or equipment, especially communications and intelligence support?"; USSOCOM J-6 Memorandum, *Collins' "SOF Report" for Congress*, 14 April 1993.

10. Guidance comes from *Joint Test Pub 3-57: Doctrine for Joint Civil Affairs Operations*, 25 October 1991; *Joint Pub 3-53: Doctrine for Joint Psychological Operations*, final coordinating draft, 11 June 1991; and from Department of the Army field manuals on those subjects.

11. Response by all regional CINCs/SOCs to the questions, "Do you have the right number and mix of SOF? Include PSYOP and CA;" comments on a draft of this report, Office of ASD SO/LIC, 7 July 1993.

12. Current status reflects response by all regional CINCs/SOCs to the question, "How smoothly do the SMUs interact with the SOC when in theater?"; Michael R. Gordon and Thomas L. Friedman, "Disastrous U.S. Raid in Somalia Nearly Succeeded, Review Finds," *New York Times*, 25 October 1993, A-1, A-10.

13. Response by all regional CINCs/SOCs to the questions, "How do you characterize relationships with USSOCOM?" and "What difference has USSOCOM made since 1987?"

14. LANTCOM J352 Memorandum, *Responsibilities of USSOCOM, SOCLANT, and J35*, 1 June 1992.

15. Roundtable discussions with LANTCOM staff and at SOCLANT, 10 June 1993; CINCLANT/SOCLANT response to the question, "Is your SOC adequately staffed?"

16. Memorandum, *Roles, Missions, and Functions of the Armed Forces of the United States*, p. 1 of attachment entitled "Secretary of Defense Decisions," signed by the Secretary of Defense, 15 April 1993; memorandum for the Commander in Chief, U.S. Atlantic Command, *Implementation Plan for USLANTCOM as the Joint Force Integrator*, 11 May 1993; "USACOM Will Assign Joint Forces, Run Joint Training," *Defense Daily*, 8 October 1993, 50.

17. Discussion with Admiral Paul David Miller, 10 June 1993, supplemented by 32 slides; CINCLANT/SOCLANT response to the question, "What is the SOF exercise program?"

18. Roundtable discussion with LANTCOM staff and at SOCLANT, 10 June 1993; CINCLANT/SOCLANT response to the question, "What is the SOF exercise program?"; LANTCOM J5 Memorandum, *USCINCLANT Programs Supporting Democracy*, 1 June 1993.

19. Roundtable discussion with LANTCOM staff and at SOCLANT, 10 June 1993; CINCLANT/SOCLANT answers to the question, "Do you have the right number and mix of SOF?"

20. *Comments on Mr. Collins' SOF Report*, memorandum by Commander, SOCCENT, 13 July 1993.

21. Ibid.; SOCCENT answer to the question, "What is the SOC's wartime authorized strength....?"; Congress, Senate, *National Defense Authorization Act for Fiscal Year 1993*, Rpt. 102-352, Committee on Armed Services, 102d Cong., 2d sess., 31 July 1992, 277.

22. Roundtable discussion with CENTCOM staff, 9 June 1993; CENTCOM answer to the question, "Do you have the right number and mix of SOF?"; David Evans, "An Impressive—Yet Troubling—Marine on Duty in Somalia," *Chicago Tribune*, 8 January 1993, 23.

23. Roundtable discussions with CENTCOM staff and at SOCCENT, 9 June 1993; CENTCOM Fact Paper, *Visit by Mr.Collins...SOF Support to CENTCOM Study*, 7 June 1993; CENTCOM Point Paper, *USCENTCOM Use of SOF Capabilities*, undated; SOCCENT response to question, "What is the SOF exercise program?"; Gordon and Friedman.

24. Discussion with Major General Waldo D. Freeman, the CENTCOM Deputy Commander in Chief, 9 June 1993, and roundtable with SOCCENT, same date.

25. *USEUCOM in the 90's*, SOCEUR slide 10, 19 June 1992.

26. Response by SOCEUR to the question, "Do you have the right number and mix of SOF?"; *USEUCOM in the 90's*, SOCEUR slides 2 and 13.

27. Response by SOCEUR to the questions, "What is the SOF exercise program?" and "How much aviation...is routinely available for exercises?"; ECSO J-4 memorandum, *Theater Airlift Status*, 6 April 1993.

28. *USEUCOM in the 90's*, SOCEUR briefing slides 2 and 13.

29. Response by SOCEUR to the questions, "Do you have the right number and mix of SOF?", "Is your SOF adequately staffed?", and "Is theater army support for SOF sufficient and responsive?"

30. Response by SOCEUR to the questions, "Does the CINC's staff have a J-3 SOD?" and "Is your SOC adequately staffed?"

31. Locher and Stiner, B-6; SOCSOUTH response to the questions, "What interoperability problems exist between SOF and conventional forces in your AOR?" and "How much SOF aviation...is routinely available for exercises?"

32. SOCSOUTH response to the question, "What is the SOF exercise program?"

33. SOCSOUTH response to the question, "Which of the nine specific SOF missions in *Title 10, USC* are most important to your command?"

34. Ibid.; Neil C. Livingstone, "Cartels of Terrorism," *Sea Power*, October 1992, 41-42.

35. Locher and Stiner, B 8-9; CINCPAC/SOCPAC response to the questions, "Do you have the right number and mix of SOF?"

36. CINCPAC/SOCPAC answers to the questions, "Do you have the right numbers and mix of SOF?" "What arrangements exist for USSOCOM to provide SOC augmentation packets in emergency?" and "If the SOC forms or becomes a JSOTF, who provides augmentation?"

37. CINCPAC/SOCPAC answers to the questions, "Do you have the right numbers and mix of SOF?" "What is the SOF exercise program?" "What interoperability problems exist between SOF and conventional forces in your AOR?" and "How much SOF aviation is routinely available?"

38. Locher and Stiner, B-9; SOC-K response to the question, "What difference has USSOCOM made since 1987?"

39. SOC-K response to the questions, "Is your SOC adequately staffed?" and "What arrangements exist for USSOCOM to provide SOF augmentation packets in emergency?"

40. SOC-K response to the question, "Do you have the right number and mix of SOF?"

41. SOC-K response to the question, "If the SOC forms or becomes a JSOTF, who provides augmentation?"

VI. Current Employment Practices

Special Operations Forces capabilities are appreciably better in 1993 than they were before Congress enacted the first SO/LIC legislation in 1986. U.S. defense decisionmakers employ these capabilities daily around the world during peacetime and war to pursue political-military missions that no other instruments of the U.S. Government could accomplish as well at any cost. More than 2,500 U.S. SOF personnel typically serve in over 40 foreign countries on any given date (figure 6).[1]

SOF encounter problems such as poverty, disease, starvation, political/economic instability, ethnic/tribal conflicts, insurgencies, narcotrafficking, terrorism, and weapon proliferation. SOF responses are to train and advise foreign armed forces in essential tactics and techniques; provide special intelligence, communications, and logistic support; conduct civil affairs and psychological operations; participate in humanitarian and disaster relief actions in the United States as well as overseas; interdict drug smugglers; reconnoiter and, when directed, take direct military action against enemies, independently or in concert with other U.S. and coalition forces.[2]

Pathfinding

"Pathfinding" is neither a primary nor a collateral SOF mission, but it nevertheless is a beneficial byproduct of the ceaseless search for new ways to excel. The military special operations community frequently serves as a "test bed" for innovative ideas, then passes findings and products on to conventional forces for adaptation and

Figure 6. *Typical SOF deployments*

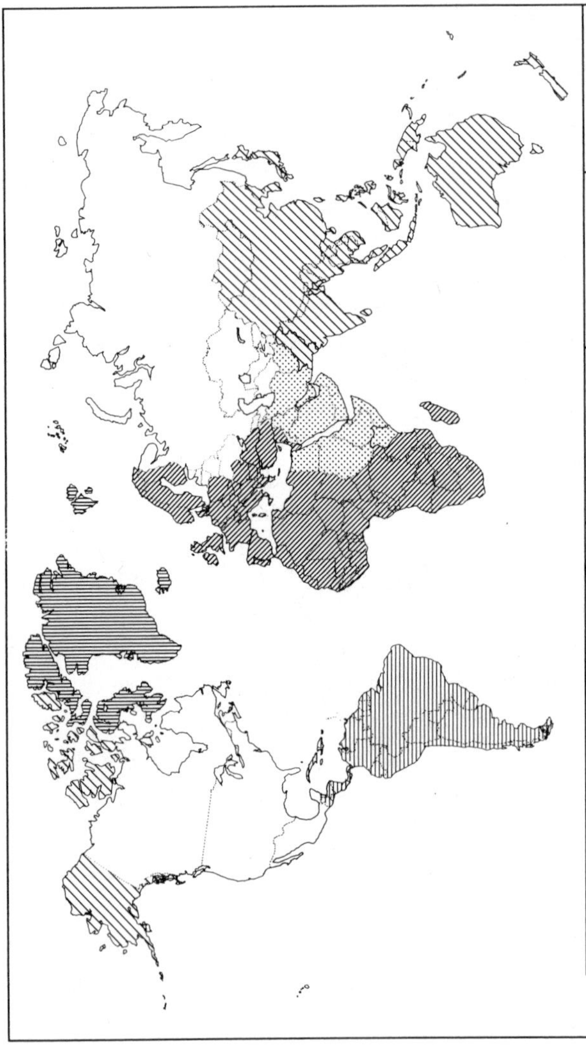

WEEK OF: 1993 30 JAN – 6 FEB	MISSIONS	PERSONNEL	COUNTRIES	STATES
CONUS	36	844	1	20
PACOM AOR	25	568	9	2
EUCOM AOR	24	381	8	
CENTCOM AOR	9	423	5	
LANTCOM AOR	8	80	3	
SOUTHCOM AOR	49	221	14	
TOTAL	151	2517	40	22

further development.[3]

ASD SO/LIC and USSOCOM, for example, promoted joint and combined doctrine that fully integrates SOFSOF with conventional forces. The special operations community has pioneered high-performance, portable communications and command center improvement programs with state-of-the-art audio-visual, information processing, and C^3 equipment. The Special Operations Command Research, Analysis, and Threat Evaluation System (SOCRATES) provides detailed intelligence to SOF everywhere. SOF aviators established the standard for night vision goggles. SOF aircraft proved the value of airborne Global Positioning Systems well before conventional forces installed GPS. Commercial Hughes 500-series helicopters, modified with SOF-peculiar subsystems and called "Little Birds," filled obvious voids during U.S. convoy escort operations in the Persian Gulf (1987-88). The Special Operations Forces Planning and Rehearsal System (SOFPARS), in development despite budgetary restrictions, seems to have widespread applications.[4]

Peacetime Engagement

Peacetime engagement applies political, military, economic, and other instruments of national power to promote regional stability, diminish threats, facilitate combat operations if deterrence fails, foster post-crisis recovery, and otherwise enhance U.S. security. Peacetime engagements employ military forces, but not military force. SOF are especially well suited, because they deter aggression primarily through good deeds, whereas conventional forces promise military retaliation. Low-key SOF maximize U.S. influence in selected countries through military-to-military contacts, information programs, and civic actions; minimize prospects of unpleasant surprise by conducting special reconnaissance missions; and garner good will in the aftermath of natural catastrophes and armed conflicts by taking care of afflicted peoples[5] (see table 4 for a few post-*Desert Storm* vignettes that affected U.S. foreign policy in a positive way):[6]

■ A Special Mission Unit early in 1993 provided counterterrorism training, equipment, and weapons to help security forces in the Republic of Georgia protect President Eduard Shevardnadze against assassination and abduction. Georgian CT specialists also received training at Fort Bragg, NC.

Table 4. Peacetime engagements and contingencies, 1990-1993

	SOCEUR		SOCPAC	SOCCENT	SOCSOUTH	SOCLANT
	Europe	Africa				
Contingency Operations	CIS Lebanon Syria Turkey Yugoslavia	Angola Algeria Cameroon Chad Ghana Liberia Libya Niger Nigeria Somalia Togo Zaire Zimbabwe	Cambodia North Korea Philippines	Iraq Kenya Kuwait Somalia	Bolivia Colombia Peru	Cuba Haiti

Peacetime Engagements (see page 99 for description)	SOCEUR		SOCPAC	SOCCENT	SOCSOUTH	SOCLANT
	Europe	Africa				
	Austria		Australia	Bahrain	Argentina*	Antigua
	Belgium	Italy	Bangladesh	Egypt	Bolivia	Barbuda
	Czecho-slovakia	Luxembourg	Hong Kong	Ethiopia	Brazil *	Bahamas
	Denmark	Netherlands	India	Jordan	Chile	Barbados
	France	Norway	Indonesia	Kenya	Colombia*	Dominica
	Germany	Poland	Japan	Kuwait	Ecuador *	Dominican Republic
	Greece	Spain	Malaysia	Pakistan	El Salvador	Grenada
	Hungary	United Kingdom	Philippines	Qatar	Guatemala	Jamaica
	Israel	Botswana	Singapore	Saudi Arabia	Honduras	Trinidad & Tobago
		Burundi	Thailand	Somalia	Panama	St. Kitt
		Cameroon		United Arab Emirates	Paraguay *	St. Lucia
		Ivory Coast			Peru	St. Vincent
		Malawi			Uruguay *	
		Namibia			Venezuela*	
		Nigeria				
		Senegal				
		Sierra Leone				
		Zimbabwe				

* SOCLANT involved in naval activities

- Army, Navy, and Air Force SOF succored thousands of Kurdish refugees in 1991, when perhaps 2,000 per day were dying in mountains along the border between Iraq and Turkey. At Cucurka Camp, where local doctors triaged 250 children and declared them hopeless, SOF medics saved all but three.[7]

- Civil affairs specialists entered Kuwait City on liberation day in 1991. Together with Kuwaiti counterparts, they directed the delivery of emergency food, water, and medical supplies to the civilian population, then assisted the Government of Kuwait in actions to restore health, sanitation, transportation, and education facilities, repair utilities, reestablish police forces, and extinguish fires in neighboring oil fields.

- A SOF team of four doctors, three nurses, and one corpsman inoculated 60,000 Cameroon citizens in 10 days during a meningitis epidemic. The cost was minuscule, because a U.S. pharmaceutical company donated vaccines that otherwise would have expired.

- Special Operations Forces in East Africa teach game wardens how to stop poachers, which enhances political, economic, and social stability in afflicted countries that derive a good deal of hard currency from tourists who come to see wild animals in their natural habitat.

- SOF personnel proficient in Russian facilitated the safe passage of U.S. military cargo aircraft through restricted air corridors during Operation *Provide Hope*, which delivered food and medical supplies to newly independent republics within the Commonwealth of Independent States (CIS) in 1991.

- SOF assisted relief efforts in Bangladesh after Cyclone Marian devastated that country in 1991 and performed similar services to help Dade County, FL, residents recover from Hurricane Andrew the following year. The resulting good will was worth a lot.

18. A combat swimmer with a closed circuit mixed-gas SCUBA investigates a submerged cable.

19. SEALs place demolition charges on an ocean-front target.

20. HC-130 Combat Shadows refuel a pair of Pave Low helicopters at night.

21. Night-vision goggles give Army and Air Force SOF aircrews a great advantage.

22. Motorcycles give Army Special Forces great mobility in the desert.

23. An Army Special Forces weapons sergeant takes aim at an unsuspecting enemy.

24. An Army Special Forces medical sergeant treats a wounded comrade deep in hostile territory.

25. Isolated villagers in Latin America welcome much needed care by Civil Affairs dentists.

26. A Civil Affairs reservist in Thailand tests well water for contamination as part of a sanitation appraisal.

27. A custom-made "ghillie suit" camouflages a Special Mission Unit sniper.

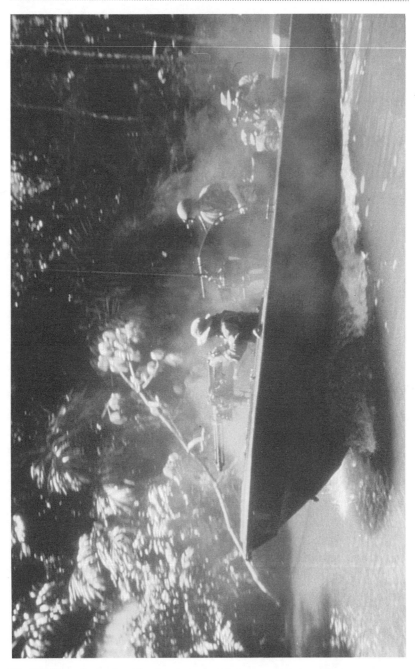

28. SEALs aboard a Boston whaler light patrol boat (PBL) practice riverine warfare.

29. Cyclone class ships, such as the Hurricane shown here, afford
SEALs long-range mobility.

30. PSYOP specialists use a portable loudspeaker to help Thai soldiers address civilian audiences.

31. PSYOP teams use "Humvee"-mounted loudspeakers to assist relief efforts after Hurricane Andrew hits Florida in 1992.

Crises and Other Contingencies

Many events involve U.S. Special Operations Forces in military confrontations that occasionally culminate in armed combat, as contingencies noted on table 3 reflect. Some, such as war with Iraq, have been well publicized, while others remain classified. A typical range of capabilities, however, is evident in the activities of Operation *Desert Storm*:

- Low-flying Pave Low helicopter crews equipped with night vision devices opened the shooting war during the early hours of 17 January 1991, when attack helicopters demolished Iraqi early warning radars.

- Skilled linguists accompanied more than 100 allied formations to facilitate coordination with non-English-speaking forces on U.S. flanks, arranged U.S. air strikes, and reduced the likelihood of casualties from "friendly fire."

- Army SOF collected intelligence, designated targets for U.S. aircraft using laser "pointers," searched for mobile SCUD missile launchers, severed enemy land lines of communication, helped organize resistance inside Kuwait, and destroyed suspected terrorist safe houses in Kuwait City. Soil samples they provided the U.S. Army's VII Corps identified surfaces that would support armored traffic.

- SEALs conducted raids, reconnaissance, and deception operations. They also cleared many small islands and oil rigs off the coast of Kuwait and destroyed a number of naval mines.

- Aircraft manned by crews skilled at clandestine infiltration and exfiltration participated in most special operations that penetrated hostile territory, acting as the principal resource to rescue downed fliers who otherwise would have fallen into enemy hands.[8]

- PSYOP leaflets and radio broadcasts helped to undermine the morale of Iraqi soldiers, provided instructions on how to surrender, instilled confidence that prisoners would be treated humanely, and provided advance warning of coalition air attacks, thus encouraging desertion."[9]

Urban combat in Somalia (autumn 1993) posed dissimilar challenges and produced less auspicious results. Special Mission Units and Rangers failed to apprehend warlord Aideed after forces allegedly under his command killed 24 Pakistani peacekeepers in June 1993. They did, however, capture 19 of Aideed's followers, including trusted lieutenants during a daring daylight raid on 3 October. The firefight that followed left 18 elite U.S. SOF dead and 73 wounded. Casualties were several times higher on the Somali side, but the tactical U.S. "victory" became a psychological defeat. President Clinton, in response to adverse public opinion at home and abroad, promised to withdraw all U.S. armed forces from Somalia by 31 March 1994. SOF departed in October 1993, and U.S. troops that remained were relegated to defensive roles.[10]

Notes

1. James R. Locher III and General Carl W. Stiner, *United States Special Operations Forces: Posture Statement*, Washington, Assistant Secretary of Defense (SO/LIC), 1993, 3-4; Major General Sidney Shachnow, "Intercultural Communication: The Need for Conceptual Skills," *Special Warfare*, February 1993, 20-22; Colonel Thomas M. Beres, *Special Operations and National Military Strategy*, a Course V Paper (Washington, DC: National War College, 1993), 8-24.

2. *Special Operations Forces, Strategic Potential*, USSOCOM slides, undated.

3. Response by John Roberts, Betac Corporation, to the question, "What can SOF do that no one else can?"

4. USSOCOM J5-0 memorandum, *Collins' "SOF Report for Congress"*, 13 April 1993; USSOCOM J6-0 memorandum, same title, 6 April 1993.

5. Captain John F. Sandoz (USN), memorandum, *The Environment Short of War and a Proposed Policy for Peacetime Engagement*, Washington, ASD SO/LIC, undated; *A Special Operations Command Perspective on Peacetime Engagement*, draft, USSOCOM, undated.

6. Locher and Stiner, 15-26; *Strategic Potential Presentation*, USSOCOM, Fort Bragg, NC, 29-31 March 1993, 28-33, 36, 40-45; Bill Gertz, "U.S. Aids Shevardnadze Guards: Special Forces Secretly Sent to Help Keep Georgian Leader in Power," *Washington Times*, 13 July 1993,

A1, A6.

7. SOF medics, who have extraordinary capabilities applicable in peacetime as well as war, are largely unsung. For a concise overview, see *SOF Medical Roles in Humanitarian Assistance Operations*, USSOCOM Command Surgeon and Political Advisor, 24 June 1993, 47 slides.

8. Locher and Stiner, 21-22; *Strategic Potential Presentation*, 17-26; "The Persian Gulf War: Schwarzkopf Answers to Reporters' Questions," *Washington Post*, 28 February 1991, 36; Tony Capaccio, "A Barrage of Commando Missions Crippled Saddam," *Defense Week*, 8 April 1991, 1, 7, 12, 13; Bill Gerz, "U.S. Commandos Steal Into Iraq to Spot Mobile Missiles," *Washington Times*, 25 January 1991, B-1.

9. *Conduct of the Persian Gulf War: Final Report to Congress* (Washington, DC: Department of Defense, 1992), J 20-21.

10. *Military Operations in Somalia: Message from the President of the United States Transmitting a Report on the Military Operations in Somalia* (Washington, DC: GPO, 1993); Raymond W. Copson, *Somalia: Operation* Restore Hope *and* UNOSOM II, IB 92131 (Washington, DC: Congressional Research Service, updated 1994); Major General Thomas Montgomery, "Command in Somalia Was Direct, Tight," *Army Times*, 22 November 1993, 28.

VII. Present and Potential Problems

The Office of the ASD SO/LIC and U.S. Special Operations Command are still experiencing "growing pains." Present and potential problems that seem to call for early attention occupy four categories: planning, programming, and budgeting; personnel management; readiness; and employment practices.

Planning, Programing, and Budgeting

The Assistant Secretary of Defense for Special Operations and Low-Intensity Conflict, the Commander in Chief of United States Special Operations Command, component commanders, and all their staffs participate in planning, programming, and budgeting processes. Results are much better than those obtained before Congress mandated reforms, but there is room for improvement. Critics most often cite the following issues.

ASD SO/LIC Responsibilities

Congress created a dichotomy in 1986 when it assigned special operations and low-intensity conflict responsibilities to the ASD SO/LIC,[1] because those two fields of endeavor are quite different in several respects. Special operations constitute *unique capabilities* that U.S. leaders may employ independently or in conjunction with other components of national power to achieve assorted objectives. Military and paramilitary SOF are the primary implements. Low-intensity conflicts, in contrast, are *political, military, economic, and/or psychological conflagrations* that occur in the twilight zone between peace and war. Many[2] departments and agencies of the U.S. Government participate in LICs. Competition among U.S. military services for attention and funds is ferocious, and respective responsibilities for peacekeeping, security assistance, humanitarian assistance, and narcoconflict raise contentious issues.[3]

Title 10, United States Code, specifies that the ASD SO/LIC "shall have as his principal duty the overall supervision (including policy and resources) of special operations activities," shall be "the principal civilian advisor to the Secretary of Defense" on such matters and, after the Secretary of Defense and Deputy, "be the principal special operations...official within the senior management of the Department of Defense." A detailed charter, prepared in response to P.L. 100-180, directs the ASD (among other duties) to prepare special operations plans and implementation guidance for selected regions around the world; to review special operations aspects of contingency plans; to oversee the readiness of SOF within U.S. unified commands; and especially to supervise the preparation of special operations programs/budgets, then help CINCSOC present proposals to Congress.[4] Statutorily imposed LIC responsibilities increase that workload, generate requirements for a larger staff, encourage jurisdictional disputes, and, to a considerable extent, duplicate the efforts of other ASDs.

Some observers conclude that SO/LIC together is too much for any one office to handle.[5] A second school of thought contends, however, that special operations and low-intensity conflict are "inextricably linked." One office with "overarching responsibility for LIC problem solving and oversight of [SOF] that almost always have a role to play" facilitates community efforts. Special operators would become increasingly isolated if SO/LIC responsibilities split. Interdepartmental and interagency contacts would wither. Opportunities for LIC policymakers and planners to overlook or overestimate SOF potential would increase. The five officers now devoted exclusively to low-intensity conflict (on an ASD staff that totals 77) consequently seem a small price to pay in anticipation of large returns, as proponents of present arrangements see it.[6]

Those two views affect very differently the desired qualifications of future ASDs, the organization of their office, and the size of their staff (five officers dedicated to LIC, for example, may not be enough to satisfy *Title 10* prescriptions as Congress originally intended). Early decisions to stand pat or adjust therefore seem desirable.

Professional Advice for ASD SO/LIC

A Special Operations Review Group investigated causes of failure after U.S. forces failed to rescue hostages from Iranian radicals in April 1980. Its members, in the so-called Holloway Report, "recommended that the Joint Chiefs of Staff give careful consideration to the establishment of a Special Operations Advisory Panel, composed of a group of carefully selected high-ranking officers (active and/or retired) who have career backgrounds in special operations or who have served at the CINC or JCS levels and who have maintained a current interest in special operations or defense policy matters." The purpose was to provide "the most objective, independent review possible" of special operations plans.[7]

DoD informally established a Special Operations Policy Advisory Group (SOPAG) in August 1983. It subsequently was chartered under provisions of P.L.. 92-46, "The Federal Advisory Committee Act," on December 20, 1983. The purpose, somewhat broader than the Holloway Report recommended, was "to assure that [SOF] revitalization efforts have the full benefit of disinterested military thinking."[8]

SOPAG members, who number 6 to 10 flag officers and civilians, have included a former Army Chief of Staff, a former Chief of Naval Operations, a former Commandant of the Marine Corps, and former CINCs. Some were skilled special operations practitioners for many years. Both ASD SO/LICs thus far confirmed, their Principal Deputies, and other civilian assistants could have benefitted greatly from their advice, but few SOPAG sessions have been as productive as the founders anticipated. Input to the SOPAG in the form of briefings by members of the ASD SO/LIC staff far exceeded the group's output. Lack of focus further reduced benefits.[9]

The ASD has not chaired the SOPAG since November 1990, so as to "revitalize" and redirect activities of that Group, broaden its expertise "through the influx of new members," more clearly identify it "as an advisory committee to the Secretary of Defense and to diminish the perception that it is principally a conduit for the policy agenda of the ASD (SO/LIC)." The SOPAG, chaired by Lieutenant General Samuel V. Wilson, U.S. Army (Ret), thereafter met several times with the Secretary of Defense until November 1992, with "encouraging results." It has not convened since, and no meeting had been scheduled as late as January 1994.[10]

SOF-Specific Support

USSOCOM has concluded Memoranda of Agreement (MOA) with U.S. military services to allocate respective responsibilities concerning planning, programming, budgeting, the execution of Major Force Program-11, and other support. MOAs with the Army and Air Force define the term "SOF-peculiar" so loosely that debates develop about such mundane matters as who should pay for common ammunition. Is it SOF-peculiar if USSOCOM requires more than the services normally allocate to conventional combat units? Do USSOCOM's special priorities make it SOF-peculiar? Other commodities cause similar controversies.[11]

The MOA between USSOCOM and the Navy, in contrast, subscribes to the official definition of SOF-peculiar: "equipment, materials, supplies, and services for which there is no broad conventional force requirement."[12] CINCSOC programs, budgets, and executes MFP-11 resources in support of NSW forces and SOC components, including common ammunition. The Chief of Naval Operations programs and budgets for major maintenance (as stipulated in Navy manuals). He also repairs real property.[13]

Whether the USSOCOM-Navy Memorandum of Agreement should be used as a model for MOAs with the Army and Air Force is a complex and contentious issue. Some applaud its simplicity. USSOCOM's Judge Advocate believes that "it impermissibly extends USCINCSOC's responsibility into Base Operating Support...[and] provides a blueprint for the total abrogation of service responsibility to USSOCOM and its components."[14]

Additive End Strengths

The Army, Navy, and the Air Force funded special operations and conventional forces through Major Force Program (MFP)-2 before congressional legislation created USSOCOM, gave CINCSOC Head of Agency authority, decreed that CINCSOC should submit program recommendations and budget proposals to the Secretary of Defense, and directed him to exercise authority, direction, and control over the expenditure of funds for all assigned forces. MFP-11 has been the source of funds for SOF ever since.[15]

On 1 December 1989 the Deputy Secretary of Defense approved a policy guidance document that gave CINCSOC authority to plan for and program SOF manpower. The Army must add to its authorized conventional personnel strength any increase in Army SOF since that date. The Navy and Air Force must do likewise (each service may also subtract any reductions). MFP-11 military manpower was "fenced" for budgeting and execution purposes. Then on 13 December 1989 the Deputy Secretary of Defense approved an initial transfer of SOF funds from service accounts to USSOCOM Defense Agency Appropriation accounts and "crosswalked" associated outyear funds. A 29 October 1990 revision to the 1 December 1989 memorandum directed CINCSOC to handle civilian manpower funding in the same way as military personnel. Current fiscal guidance, dated 24 February 1992, restated CINCSOC's "sole authority for adjusting MILPERS resources in accordance with his direction and [Memoranda of Agreement] with the Military Departments."[16]

"Additive end strength" policies have caused no serious problems yet. Dissension between USSOCOM and the Services could develop, however, if the U.S. special operations community expands significantly to accommodate an increasing number of missions while conventional forces and accompanying funds experience further reductions.

Personnel Management

The small U.S. special operations community experiences some unique personnel problems. The following expositions single out four that have far- reaching ramifications, or soon could.

USSOCOM Battle Staffs

Every theater special operations command (SOC) currently relies extensively on reserve component augmentation packets for major exercises and emergencies. All eagerly await the formation of USSOCOM Battle Staffs.[17]

Two battle rosters list primary and alternate active duty personnel who are assigned to USSOCOM Headquarters. Members of the first roster must be ready to deploy within 24 hours after notification. They possess operations, intelligence, communications, logistics, and other skills that theater SOCs are known to need most. The maximum number ready to surge is 29. Alternates and selected personnel from USSOCOM's component commands constitute the second roster, whose members could fill additional requests for not more than 29 commissioned and noncommissioned officers. They prepare to follow within one week. Anticipated capabilities, however, will not be available until USSOCOM acquires sufficient weapons and makes them immediately available for use by personnel on the two battle rosters.[18]

Some critics contend that USSOCOM Headquarters is overstaffed, and therefore should permanently transfer a good many SOF officers and NCOs to undermanned theater SOCs. An intensive survey by the U.S. Army Force Integration Support Agency failed to settle disputes, which continue.[19]

Career Opportunities

Career opportunities for U.S. SOF vary from better than average to poor, depending on present rank, Service idiosyncrasies, and specialties. Rear admirals, Air Force major generals, Air Force helicopter pilots, and Army Special Forces officers encounter "glass promotion ceilings." SEALs and Reserve Component CA/PSYOP officers, who are few in number and in constant demand, find little time to attend military schools and colleges. SOF in several categories find assignment potential quite limited. Section 167(e)(2)(J) of *Title 10 United States Code* tells CINCSOC to monitor such matters, which are parent Service responsibilities, but he has little ability to reverse adverse trends.

Flag officers. SOF-qualified flag officers from a multiservice pool of candidates ideally should compete for every senior command and staff position within USSOCOM Headquarters, its component commands, and theater SOCs. However, a relatively small reservoir now exists, partly because SOF generals and admirals find it difficult to progress within the special operations community after they pin on the first star, partly because non-SOF officers fill many key slots.

The SOF community currently is authorized 20 flag officers, a favorable number compared with conventional forces, but the Commanding General of U.S. Army Special Operations Command at Fort Bragg, NC, occupies the only three-star billet (USSOCOM's Deputy Commander in Chief wears two). AFSOC rates a major general, although a three- or four-star officer leads every other Air Force major command. The most senior SEAL occupies a two-star space on the USSOCOM staff. A rear admiral (lower half) heads NAVSPECWARCOM. Army flag officers accordingly can reach the top of the promotion ladder as SOF and compete for assignment as CINCSOC; Navy and Air Force officers cannot. Theoretically they may attain three-star rank by returning temporarily to parent services, but in practice chances are poor, because they are considered too specialized or "out of touch."[20]

The Navy has an officer career field that fosters first-class SOF. Occupants constitute a solid professional core that excludes "outsiders" lacking Naval Special Warfare expertise. Promotions to flag rank are more than twice the fleet percentages; SEALs who become admirals normally have served 20 years or more at progressive levels, from platoon through NSW group. Two disadvantages exist, however: Progression stops at two stars, although experience could continue to pay off if spaces were authorized; and the two SOF admirals, who must fill both specified billets, can never serve as a SOC commander or on the Joint Staff, where their expertise would be welcome.[21]

Army Generals appointed as CINCSOC have graduated from the Joint Special Operations Command, the Ranger Regiment, and/or the 82d Airborne Division. Their experience emphasized direct action missions. Army Special Forces generals are stymied after they acquire a second star; the only one who served in any SOF capacity as a lieutenant general was William P. Yarborough, a personal favorite of President Kennedy. No active duty PSYOP or Civil Affairs fficer has ever become a brigadier general.[22]

Most Air Force generals in SOF command and staff positions arrive mainly via conventional routes. Few SOF careerists with experience at several levels ever wear stars. The current Commander of Air Force Special Operations Command accumulated 1 year with an Air Commando Squadron in Vietnam and 4 months with JSOC before attaining flag rank. AFSOC's most recent Vice Commander flew Combat Talons for a year in Vietnam. His replacement logged no SOF time before assignment and neither did Air Force major generals who recently served as USSOCOM's Deputy CINC or as J-5 (policies, plans, and doctrine). There also is a tendency for Air Force generals in SOF assignments to retire as one-star officers, which leaves few upwardly mobile role models like the last Deputy Commander of the Joint Special Operations Command, who won the Air Force Cross and two Silver Stars as a helicopter pilot.[23]

Service idiosyncracies. Some personnel management practices below flag rank adversely affect current and future capabilities in

USSOCOM's Army, Navy, and Air Force components.

■ Army problems center on Special Forces (SF), the most versatile of all SOF. SF officers have belonged to a separate branch since 1987, because extensive study determined they require unique career progression paths. Each, for example, must qualify first in some basic branch such as infantry, armor, or artillery *and thereafter* become proficient at SF skills. *Then* they command units, attend prescribed schools, and satisfy joint duty demands like other Army officers. SF professionals additionally must master the geography, culture, language, political-economic-social-military context and problems of a particular foreign area, and establish key personal contacts (usually in several countries). The small SF branch moreover must fill many billets at USSOCOM Headquarters, on the staffs of five regional CINCs, with six theater SOCs, and with Special Operations Coordination Elements SOCOORDS) that are planned for each Army corps. As a result, SF officers are hard pressed to compete with conventional peers for attendance at senior service colleges, because identical selection criteria apply to all despite inordinately high demands on SF time. Lieutenant colonels who never commanded a SF company often command SF battalions. Only 5 of the past 21 SF Group commanders have become brigadier generals, compared with 3 out of 5 in Delta and 5 out of 5 in the Ranger Regiment. Prospects for early improvement seem slight, because the SF Branch, which never attained its authorized personnel strength, has lost officers to personnel reductions and selective early release programs at a percentage rate more than twice that of infantry. As a consequence, many SF professionals feel like second-class citizens in the Army SOF community.[24]

■ Naval Special Warfare personnel management problems, which center on boat crews, are somewhat less complex than those of Amry Special Forces. Crew members, in sharp contrast with SEALSs who occupy an NSW career field, participate in each 18-month predeployment -deployment-post deployment cycle, but then resume service with the fleet just as they become fully qualified. Each succeeding cycle starts with fresh boat crews that include few or no seamen with previous SOF experience. That practice seemed satisfactory until an influx of sophisticated craft and equipment created needs for professional NSW boat crews. Increasing emphases on foreign internal defense (FID) missions, which call for foreign language proficiency, reinforce such requirements.[25]

■ Air Force officer personnel management problems below flag level center on a lack of special operations experience. The 1st Special Operations Wing at Hurlburt Field is a traditional stepping stone to brigadier general, although the last 5 commanders had never before served in a SOF squadron (only 7 out of 15 wing and group commanders since 1981 have done so). Squadron operations officers, who are lieutenant colonels, fit into much the same mold. USAF spokesmen cite the rapid expansion of AFSOC from 5 to 12 squadrons between 1988 and 1992 as a mitigating circumstance, but in February 1994 AFSOC had not yet appreciably increased the percentage of SOF professionals compared with conventional fliers.[26]

A shortage of Army and Air Force SOF commissioned officers with the full range of requisite skills will persist until new personnel management practices replace present procedures. NSW boat crews will be not reach maximum capability for similar reasons.

Minority Accessions

SOF recruiters thus far have enlisted few minorities and women, who are less well represented in USSOCOM than among conventional forces in the U.S. Army, Navy, Air Force, and Marine Corps. Rosters in mid-1993 reflected 13 percent black, 5 percent hispanic, and 5 percent female.[27] Those figures are somewhat inflated, because they include civilian employees as well as military SOF. The percentage of minority officers is much lower in USSOCOM Headquarters and every component command (less than one percent in NAVSPECWARCOM).[28] Few minorities spontaneously seek SOF assignments for reasons that remain obscure. Women who presently occupy staff billets or serve with PSYOP and Civil Affairs units are highly valued. USSOCOM, however, "is firmly against the assignment of women to combat positions within its operational units" (aircrews may prove to be an exception).[29]

Readiness

High readiness standards demand active and reserve component SOF that can respond expeditiously with little or no warning whenever required and perform effectively upon arrival. The right mix of first-rate personnel, weapons, and equipment is essential. USSOCOM satisfies those criteria in most respects, as previous discussions indicate, but a few important deficiencies are evident.

Hardware

The Soviet Union and Warsaw Pact no longer threaten the United States or its allies, but the U.S. military SOF community must continually improve (in some cases replace) present hardware if it is to retain a sharp edge against lesser, unpredictable opponents who are increasingly able to wage high-tech wars.[30]

Air transportation. The finest Special Operations Forces imaginable would be impotent in the absence of sufficient long-haul airlift able to deliver them where needed in time to accomplish assigned missions. There is no certainty, however, that Air Force Mobility Command's aging fleet, which serves many purposes, will be able to meet SOF needs indefinitely. Senior officers in USSOCOM Headquarters, at every component command, and in every U.S. military service predict problems in the future unless replacements for C-141 transports are soon forthcoming.[31]

C-141s were activated in 1965 and have undergone numerous modifications to meet more specialized needs (270 were "stretched" between 1978 and 1982 and had in-flight refueling receptacles added). Ceaseless use, starting well before Operation *Desert Shield*, is taking a toll. Actual flying hours during FY 1991 were 60 percent over those programmed (442,980 vs. 275,591), and subsequent operating tempos have allowed little opportunity to recover. Aircraft and crews often land, discharge cargoes, reload, and leave. Structural cracks in wing "weep holes" that could lead to fuel leaks and weakened wings recently caused Air Force Materiel Command to reduce allowable loads by 26 percent. Fifty C-141s out of 214 currently are undergoing depot maintenance, instead of 13 as scheduled. The remaining 164 aircraft are maintaining the rates planned for 201, which further increases wear and tear. C-5 transports, which must take up the slack, are experiencing more maintenance problems than normal.[32]

There is a serious problem obtaining replenishment parts required to keep fixed-wing aircraft and helicopters in service. AFSOC acquires aircraft and initial repair parts through MFP-11, but the Air Force Stock Fund is the source of replenishment parts. This arrangement does not always work well. The Air Force lacks funds to satisfy all needs, and parts for grounded aircraft take priority over parts to fill empty shelves. More money would not immediately rectify such deficiencies, because spares for some SOF aircraft are in short supply—procurement in some cases would take 2 years. Consequently, AFSOC finds it increasingly difficult to maintain aircraft on hand, and mission effectiveness will eventually decline if those trends continue.[33]

Communications. U.S. Special Operations Forces sometimes must maintain direct contact with National Command Authorities (NCA) in Washington, DC, from remote locations overseas and often operate under isolated, clandestine conditions. Mission accomplishment and lives depend on fast, reliable, interoperable, easily transportable (preferably portable), secure communications.

Communications equipment issued through official channels or acquired through commercial purchase and improved by ingenious SOF is generally satisfactory. Ongoing actions reportedly are correcting most problems, with three exceptions:

- Four space satellites furnish the only secure communications link between forward deployed SOF and the United States, and all channels on each are fully committed. Access depends on national priorities at any given moment. Alternative means, such as HF radio, are less reliable.[34]

- CINCPAC often loads SOF on aircraft carriers en route to employment areas. Those ships "are already crowded with sophisticated C^3I suites and are sensitive to change and interference" that Special Operations Forces aboard cause when they transmit radio messages. Interoperability problems between SOF afloat and conventional forces ashore likely will continue unless the Navy installs communications equipment aboard selected aircraft carriers specifically for SOF use.[35]

- *DoD Directive 5100.3* requires the Navy to provide or arrange a signal communications package for SOCPAC; the Navy has not yet done so. U.S. Forces Korea relies on the Army 1st Signal Brigade to provide SOC-K with similar support, but the brigade lacks sufficient resources. Both SOCs experience command/control problems as a result.[36]

Research and development. Special Operations Forces have unique needs for weapons, land-sea-air transportation, communications, survival/support systems, and supplies. Masterful improvisation and off-the-shelf procurement will always be essential to some extent,[37] because special operations frequently are unpredictable, but they cannot supplant competent research and development (R&D) programs.

CINCSOC's R&D priorities emphasize individual equipment, followed by advanced standoff weapons that, for example, would improve AC-130 gunship survivability; nonlethal weapons; alternative power sources; "signature" control, including stealth; assorted sensors (especially night vision); and information warfare systems. Many near-term projects are well under way.[38] Long-range explorations, not counting the "far future," concentrate on such esoteric items as multispectral camouflage, physiological-psychological-ergonomical enhancements, hybrid surface/submarine craft, planning and rehearsal systems, and electro-optical text translators.[39] Special Mission Units want devices that can locate nuclear explosives within designated buildings then, employed by experts, disable them safely and expeditiously.[40]

The quest for excellence has always been intense, but research, development, and acquisition (RDA) problems made attainment difficult before Congress took action in 1986, because service RDA procedures did not normally accommodate small special operations programs and short-fused priorities. Individuals who helped draft the legislation that established USSOCOM envisaged a more flexible system when they made CINCSOC responsible for SOF-peculiar RDA and provided a budget for that purpose.[41]

Critics, however, contend that in some respects USSOCOM RDA procedures are too much like those of U.S. military services. Guidelines specifically designed to fill small inventories expeditiously are insufficient; links between USSOCOM's RDA specialists and SOF users allegedly are loose; and few program managers reportedly possess adequate RDA experience. Relations between J-3R (requirements), J-8 (resources), and RDA (program execution) may also need tightening. Furthermore, SOF research, development, and acquisition programs overlook some important requirements, and RDA cycles are overly long (10 to 15 years for some aircraft). Single points of contact seldom maintain responsibility and accountability for logistic support of major items from "cradle to grave." USSOCOM could initiate some useful reforms unilaterally, but DoD policies and congressional legislation that allow some exceptions to existing research, development and acquisition regulations may be needed to reduce response times and achieve desired results.[42]

Education and Training

Theater Commanders in Chief applaud USSOCOM's consistent ability to prepare and provide superb forces[43] despite "housekeeping" chores (particularly on Army posts), support for ROTC and reserve components each summer, and other duties that divert SOF from training. Two significant problems still exist, however: AFSOC does not control SOF aircrew training, and foreign language instruction fails to satisfy ever-changing requirements.

AFSOC flight instruction. Air Mobility Command currently conducts initial aircrew qualification training for AFSOC at Kirtland AFB, NM. The newly created Air Education and Training Command soon will assume responsibility if transfer plans reach fruition. USSOCOM meanwhile furnishes MFP-11 funds and AFSOC provides instructors while the Air Force exercises oversight.[44] These arrangements are contentious, because Section 167 of *Title 10, U.S. Code*, holds CINCSOC accountable for all aspects of combat readiness, including training. As it stands, conventional Air Force officers establish standards for AFSOC aircrews and rate AFSOC instructors. Renegotiation of the USSOCOM-Air Force Memorandum of Agreement with respect to training therefore seems advisable.[45]

Language training. Many members of the U.S. military establishment are fluent in common foreign languages such as French, German, and Spanish. Sufficient numbers are also well qualified Special Operations Forces. However, SOF who are conversant in local dialects—for example, Creole, which is common in Haiti—range from few to none. Some associated problems probably are correctable, others probably are not. On the bright side, better personnel management practices might screen students more carefully to ascertain motivation (strong interest must be shown to learn a language as difficult as Arabic). Graduates might more often receive assignments where they can daily apply what is learned.[46]

The U.S. intelligence community cannot always predict SOF needs, although the relevance of programs conducted by the Defense Language Institute Foreign Language Center in Monterey, CA, and by USASOC's school at Fort Bragg, NC, depends heavily on consequent requirements. Egyptian and Syrian, for example, emerged as the most important Arabic dialects after the Arab-Israeli War of 1967; as a result, only 16 Arabic linguists on active duty (less than 1percent) had studied Iraqi before Saddam Hussein invaded Kuwait. No one predicted large-scale SOF employment in Kurdistan or Somalia, where Operations *Provide Comfort* and *Restore Hope* took place. The maintenance of language skills is just as essential as initial learning, but for most linguists, peak proficiency occurs the day a diploma is received. Unrelated military duties thereafter inhibit further progression.[47]

No early solutions to SOF language training problems seem feasible. First-term enlistees commonly shed military uniforms after receiving instruction at DoD's expense. Shortages are especially severe among Reserve Component units, whose members devote most time to civilian occupations. Improvements will likely be on the margins.[48]

Reserve Components

Both Active and Reserve Component (AC, RC) forces contribute to U.S. special operations capabilities, which causes two unresolved issues to arise: Command and control and the AC/RC mix.

Command and control. All active and reserve U.S. Special Operations Forces in the United States are assigned to USSOCOM, as Section 167 (b), Title 10, U.S. Code, prescribes, unless otherwise directed by the Secretary of Defense. CINCSOC currently commands all SOF in the Army Reserve and exercises operational control over Naval Reserve SOF as codified in the Chief of Naval Operations Missions and Functions Directive (OP-NAV Instruction 5450-221B).

The Air Force Reserve, however, remains under USAF jurisdiction when not on active duty. The National Guard Bureau, which interprets the intent of *Title 10* to suit State purposes, objects to any policy that would pass control of its Army and Air Force SOF to USSOCOM.[49] CINCSOC therefore has asked the Secretary of Defense for clarification.[50] Members of the Joint Staff have concluded that "the law does not permit the Military Departments to retain peacetime [command and control] of RC forces, as the Air Force has done." Moreover, they found that "the dual status of [National Guard] forces limits the authority that combatant commanders can exercise over assigned NG forces when not on active duty but permits them to exercise training and readiness oversight...." Final disposition still awaits congressional action.[51]

Active-reserve mix. CINCSOC, his component commanders, regionally oriented CINCs, theater SOCs, and their staffs all believe an undesirable imbalance exists between Active and Reserve Component PSYOP and Civil Affairs forces, which receive important missions in almost every contingency plan and are in daily demand.[52]

Ninety-seven percent of all civil affairs units are in the U.S. Army Reserve (USAR). One active battalion at Fort Bragg, NC, chronically under its authorized personnel strength of 212, bears most of the operational load. Theater Commanders in Chief repeatedly request reserves, because the 96th CA Battalion cannot be everywhere at once and the USAR contains many civil affairs skills it cannot replicate. It is impractical to call entire reserve units when requesters need only a fraction of their capabilities. Volunteers, who are not universally well qualified, consequently fill most gaps. Recurrent active duty periods of long duration, however, cause domestic difficulties and jeopardize civilian jobs.[53]

Seventy-three percent of all military psychological operations forces reside in the U.S. Army Reserve. One active PSYOP Group at Fort Bragg, NC, currently below its authorized personnel strength of 1,137, experiences problems that are less stringent those for civil affairs.[54] The USAR contains two Army Special Forces Groups; the Army National Guard (ARNG) contains two more. None of them can match the competence of active groups (language proficiency alone is a formidable barrier). Critics, who see few reasons why RC Special Forces should be organized like active counterparts, consequently recommend a review to ascertain whether all or part of Reserve Component SF units retained for post-Cold War use should be restructured to provide A Detachments and individual replacements instead of battalions and groups.

Employment Practices

More than 2,500 U.S. SOF currently serve in 40 to 50 foreign countries on any given date (figure 6 and table 4). Some, however, are far more active than others. Mission priorities and the potential for overcommitment consequently raise serious questions.

Mission Priorities

U.S. SOF pursue 10 missions that Section 167(j), *Title 10, U.S. Code*, prescribes. Foreign internal defense (FID), humanitarian assistance, counternarcotics operations, and disaster relief currently determine SOF peacetime operating tempos. Theater CINCs and their SOCs identify direct action, counterterrorism, and special reconnaissance as their top priorities when crises occur. Combat search and rescue capabilities are essential whenever U.S. forces engage in armed combat.[55] Crises, however, have occupied only a few SOF for relatively short periods since a cease-fire terminated the shooting war with Iraq in February 1991.

Collateral missions. Special operations doctrine designates antiterrorism, security assistance, humanitarian assistance/disaster relief, counterdrug operations, personnel recovery, counterproliferation, peacekeeping, special activities, and coalition warfare as collateral missions. These decisions, which presumably influence training priorities and educational courses in military colleges/schools, correlate poorly with current peacetime and wartime requirements. So-called "non-traditional" missions indeed may become paramount for the next decade or so. Doctrine is needed, but none now exists. A review therefore seems desirable.

Paramilitary missions. *Title 10, U.S. Code*, and special operations doctrine disregard paramilitary missions. The Central Intelligence Agency retains primary responsibility, but the Drug Enforcement Administration and the State Department's Bureau of International Narcotics Matters both conduct or control highly specialized, small-scale paramilitary operations. Consolidation of paramilitary matters under CINCSOC's command might be preferable to continued diffusion.

Special Mission Units. Few dispute the desirability of a highly proficient counterterrorism joint task force. Many members of the U.S. special operations community, however, deny that Special Mission Units (SMUs) also should undertake the most sensitive and difficult reconnaissance and direct action missions. Misgivings and morale problems are most obvious among Army Special Forces but are evident throughout USSOCOM, because SMUs reportedly enjoy promotion/assignment opportunities, budgetary allocations, flying hours, ammunition allowances, joint training time, and other favors far superior to those that other SOF receive. These allegations are unconfirmable, but discontent seems so deep seated and widespread that objective investigations designed to substantiate or deny such contentions and probe resultant implications appear advisable.

Combat search and rescue. Section 167, *Title 10, U.S. Code*, assigns theater search and rescue (TSAR) responsibilities to U.S. Special Operations Command "insofar as [they] relate to special operations." CINCSOC accordingly must organize, equip, train, and provide forces that are prepared to find and recover personnel in distress on land or at sea during peacetime, contingencies, and war. Loose interpretations of the *Title 10* edict, however, cause commitments to exceed SOF capabilities.

Complete responsibility for combat search and rescue (CSAR) missions, which arise only during armed conflicts, also remains beyond reach of SOF aircraft and crews, which must perform many other tasks during crises.[56] The Chairman of the Joint Chiefs of Staff therefore recommended, and the Secretary of Defense recently directed, all U.S. military Services to conduct CSAR operations.[57] Theater CINCs, however, still rely on specialized SOF aircraft and uniquely qualified SOF crews to rescue personnel from enemy territory or denied areas wherever conventional CSAR forces seem inadequate, which is frequently. Dedicated USAF assets are beginning to bear larger CSAR loads, but *Title 10* and DoD instructions perhaps should enunciate SOF responsibilities more specifically to forestall future overloads.

Potential for Overcommitment

The present Commander in Chief of U.S. Special Operations Command and his immediate predecessor deny that SOF are overcommitted, except for the small active duty civil affairs battalion.[58] Senior SOF officers interviewed in April 1993, as well as most theater CINCs and their SOC Commanders in June 1993, expressed less optimistic opinions. They additionally singled out SOC staffs, helicopter crews, SEAL platoons, and selected Army

Special Forces units, whose members reenlist repeatedly but are approaching saturation.[59]

The root cause of such problems is too few SOF for too many tasks. That trend, which continues because senior leaders tend to say "can do" when they shouldn't, accomplishes current missions at the expense of future capabilities. A greater degree of restraint perhaps could lighten loads without slighting *essential* tasks.

The Search for Solutions

General Wayne A. Downing, in his capacity as CINCSOC, subscribes to the tenet, "Who Thinks Wins." He consequently has established an intellectual clearinghouse designed to initiate, furnish a focus for, sustain, expand, and perfect a flow of innovative ideas that could help USSOCOM solve pressing SOF problems such as those just described. The objective is to provide an open forum for previously untapped talent throughout the active, reserve, and retired SOF communities and thereby compile fresh options concerning every conceivalbe subject. The ASD SO/LIC will participate in this unique endeavor.[60]

Notes

1. Section 1311, *Public Law 99-661*, 14 November 1986.

2. For official DoD definitions of special operations and low-intensity conflict, refer to *Joint Pub 3-05: Doctrine for Joint Special Operations* (Washington, DC: Office of the Chairman, Joint Chiefs of Staff, 1992), GL-13, GL-20.

3. *Department of Defense Directives* for each Under Secretary and Assistant Secretary.

4. Section 136, *Title 10, United States Code*; Section 1211, *Public Law 100-180*, 4 December 1987; memorandum from Deputy Secretary of Defense William H. Taft IV to Senator Sam Nunn, 4 January 1988; *Department of Defense Directive 5138.3*, "Assistant Secretary of Defense (Special Operations and Low-Intensity Conflict)," 4 January 1988.

5. For some related views, see Seth Cropsey, "Barking Up a Fallen Tree: The Death of Low-Intensity Conflict," *National Interest* (Spring 1992): 53-60, and a rebuttal (Summer 1992): 109.

6. *Report on SO/LIC and SOPAG*, an ASD SO/LIC memorandum, 10 July 1993, 1-2.

7. *Rescue Mission Report* (the Holloway Report) (Washington, DC: Joint Chiefs of Staff Special Operations Review Group, 1980), 61-62.

8. *Special Operations Policy Advisory Group*, memorandum from the Principal Deputy Assistant Secretary of Defense for International Security Affairs to the Secretary of Defense, 29 August 1983; "Establishment of the Special Operations Policy Advisory Group (SOPAG)," *Federal Register* (22 December 1983): 56820.

9. Discussions with several past and present SOPAG members, as well as a former SOPAG Executive Secretary, between January and June 1993.

10. *Establishment and Subsequent Revitalization of the Special Operations Policy Advisory Group (SOPAG)*, memorandum for Mr. John Collins from the present SOPAG Executive Secretary, 23 June 1993; telephone conversation with Lt. Gen. Sam Wilson, 24 June 1993; *Report on SO/LIC and SOPAG*, 2-3, 4.

11. Memorandum from Margaret Kinkead, USSOCOM, Washington Office, 14 July 1993; roundtable discussions at USSOCOM, 28 April 1993, and at AFSOC, 27 April 1993.

12. *Joint Pub 3-05: Joint Doctrine for Special Operations*, GL-20.

13. Draft Annex A, *Memorandum of Agreement Between United States Navy and United States Special Operations Command*, 25 May 1993, 4-6; Kinkead memorandum.

14. *Mr. John Collins' Report to Congress Update*, memorandum by USSOCOM Judge Advocate, 12 July 1993, 2-5.

15. Section 1311, *P.L. 99-661*, 14 November 1986; Section 1211, *P.L. 100-180*, 4 December 1987; Section 712, *P.L. 100-456*, 29 September 1988.

16. *Background on MFP-11 Funding*, USSOCOM Washington Office memorandum, 12 May 1993.

17. Response by all CINCs/SOCs to the question, "What arrangements exist for USSOCOM to provide SOC augmentation packets in an emergency?"

18. *SOC Battle Roster*, USSOCOM memorandum, undated.

19. Executive Summary, *Manpower Requirements Evaluation Study: United States Special Operations Command* (Washington, DC: U.S. Army Force Integration Support Agency [USAFISA], 1992); *USAFISA Manpower Study Final Report*, CINCSOC memorandum to ASD SO/LIC, 29 October 1992; *USSOCOM Headquarters Manpower*, ASD SO/LIC memorandum to CINCSOC, 21 November 1992.

20. See authorized manning levels for USSOCOM Headquarters, USASOC, AFSOC, NAVSPECWARCOM, JSOC, and theater SOCs.

21. Roundtable discussions at USSOCOM Headquarters, at component command headquarters, and with Army, Navy, and Air Force SOF in the Pentagon, April 1993; John Brennen, "Special Ops Generals," *Armed Forces Journal*, July 1992.

22. Review of biographic summaries.

23. Ibid; *SOF Leadership*, USSOCOM J-3 memorandum, 8 May 1993; Glenn W. Goodman, "USAF General Officer Wanted; SOF Colonels Need Not Apply," *Armed Forces Journal*, January 1994, 37; Goodman, "The Air Force SOF Dilemma: Can An Operator Ever Make General?" *Armed Forces Journal*, February 1994, 37.

24. Major General James A. Guest, *Status of the Force: Fill the Force With Quality*, 33 slides, undated; Colonel K. L. Coughenour, memorandum for Commanding General, U.S. Army JFK Special Warfare Center and School, *After-Action Review—Special Forces Officer Branch Chief* (14 June 90-30 June 92)(Alexandria, VA: U.S. Total Army Personnel Command, 1992); roundtable discussion with Army SOF officers in the Pentagon, 20 April 1993; "RIF Board Results," *Army Times*, 21 June 1993, 14.

25. Roundtable discussions with NSW officers in the Pentagon, 23 April 1993 and at NAVSPECWARCOM, 30 April 1993.

26. Goodman, 37. Roundtable discussions with Air Force SOF officers in the Pentagon, 21 April 1993 and at AFSOC, 27 April 1993; *SOF Leadership*; USSOCOM J-3 memorandum; AFSOC *Personnel Overview*, slide, "Command (1981-Present)"; *U.S. Air Force Strategy Division (XOXS) Inputs for CRS Report to Congress on SOF*, memorandum, 13 July 1993.

27. *Minorities in USSOCOM*, USSOCOM memorandum for Washington Office, 27 May 1993.

28. *Minority Recruiting for Naval Special Warfare*, memorandum from Commander, Naval Special Warfare Command to recruiters, 8 January 1993.

29. *Women in Combat*, USSOCOM J5-0 memorandum, 21 January 1993; James C. Hyde, "DoD Gives Mixed Message on Women in Combat," *Armed Forces Journal*, June 1993, 61; roundtable discusssion with SOF officers in the Pentagon, 20 April 1993, and at AFSOC, 27 April 1993. For elaboration of related issues, see proceedings of the Special Operations Panel, Presidential Commission on the Assignment of Women in the Armed Forces, Dallas, TX, 27 August 1992.

30. *U.S. Weapons: The Low-Intensity Threat Is Not Necessarily a Low-Technology Threat*, Report NR. GAO/PEMD-90-13 (Washington,DC: U.S. General Accounting Office, 1990).

31. Roundtable discussions at USSOCOM Headquarters, USASOC, AFSOC, NAVSPECWARCOM, and JSOC, April 1993.

32. *Point Paper on Global Mobility*, HQ USAF (XOFM), 10 March 1993.

33. AFSOC memorandum to author, 29 June 1993.

34. Telephone conversation with USSOCOM J-6, 29 June 1993.

35. Ibid.; CINCPAC response to the question, "What interoperability problems exist between SOF and conventional forces in your AOR?"

36. *More Report Comments*, J-3 (SOD) memorandum, 12 July 1993.

37. Three USSOCOM memoranda, *Collins' "SOF Report for Congress,"* identify 20 distinctive examples of improvisation and commercial purchase: Director, Special Operations Research, Development, and Acquisition Center, 13 April 1993; Director, Psychological Operations and Civil Affairs, same date; Director of Command, Control, Communications, Computers, and Information Systems, J6, 6 April 1993.

38. James R. Locher III and General Carl W. Stiner, *United States Special Operations Forces: Posture Statement* (Washington, DC: Assistant Secretary of Defense [SO/LIC], 1993), C8-12; James C. Hyde, "SOCOM R&D Focus Shifts Toward the Individual Warrior," *Armed Forces Journal*, July 1993, 29-30.

39. Gary L. Smith, *SOF Systems for Tomorrow*, USSOCOM Acquisition Executive Briefing, 9 slides, 1 March 1993.

40. Capt. Paul Shemella (USN), "Defusing Mega Weapons Aim of Revised Doctrine," *National Defense*, January 1994, 33-34; Tony Capaccio, "Commando Role in Countering Renegade Nukes Will Grow," *Defense Week*, 20 December 1993, 5. Roundtable discussion with Special Mission Unit officers at Fort Bragg, NC, 26 April 1993; Earl Lane, "Way to Zap Terrorist N-Bomb?" *Long Island Newsday*, 5 May 1993, 17.

41. Section 167(e) (1) (G) and (f), *P.L. 99-661*, 14 November 1986.

42. Peter Bahnsen, *Research, Development, and Acquisition*, memorandum, 28 June 1993; Al Danis, *Special Operations Acquisition Process*, memorandum, 22 June 1993; Commander Walter Pullar, *Naval Special Warfare (NSW) Research, Development, and Acquisition (RDA) Problems*, undated memorandum (June 1993),

43. Responses by regionally oriented CINCs and theater SOCs to the question, "What difference has USSOCOM made since 1987?"

44. *AFSOC Initial Training at Kirtland*, USSOCOM J-3 memorandum, 5 May 1993; *Training Support Issues for AFSOC Aircrews*, message from CINCSOC to AFSOC, 4 May 1993.

45. Ibid.; roundtable, 21 April 1993.

46. Sergeant First Class Kenneth C. Dawe, "Police Call, Guard Duty Won't Keep Up Vital Language Skills," *Army*, July 1993, 13-14; "The Linguistic Gap," letters to the editor by Julie M. Holden and William C. Burrow, *Army*, September 1992, 6, 8.

47. Major James C. McNaughton, "Can We Talk?," *Army*, June 1992, 21-24, 26, 28.

48. Discussions at USASOC, 26 April 1993 and at USSOCOM, 28 April 1993; Congress, House, *Defense Language Institute Foreign Language Center*, Hearings Before the Investigations Subcommittee of the Committee on Armed Services, 102d Cong., 2d sess., 27 May 1993; Cpt. Elizabeth A. C. Popowski, "Reserve Linguists," *Army*, November 1993, 4-5.

49. J-3 memorandum for Chairman of the Joint Chiefs of Staff, *Report on Assignment of Special Operations Forces*, 18 May 1993.

50. CINCSOC memorandum through the Chairman of the Joint Chiefs of Staff to the Secretary of Defense, *Command and Control of Reserve and National Guard Special Operations Forces*, 13 January 1993.

51. J-3 memorandum for the Chairman of the Joint Chiefs of Staff, *Report on Assignment of Special Operations Forces*; telephonic status report from J-3 (SOD), 30 June 1993; William Matthews, "Move Would Strengthen Reserves, *Army Times*, 27 September 1993, 20; Rick Maze, "Shali Voices Concern on Separate Commands, *Army Times*, 4 October 1993, 24.

52. Roundtable discussions with, or correspondence from, all sources mentioned in text paragraph.

53. Locher and Stiner, B-2; discussion with Lieutenant General Wayne A. Downing, 26 April 1993; telephone conversation with the Acting Chief of Staff, Civil Affairs and Psychological Command, 1 July 1993.

54. Telephone conversation, 1 July 1993.

55. Response by theater CINCs/SOCs to the question, "Which of the nine specific missions in *Title 10, United States Code* are most important to your command?"

56. *Joint Pub 3-05: Doctrine for Joint Special Operations*, Washington, DC: Office of the Chairman, Joint Chiefs of Staff, 28 October 1992, II 12-15.

57. *Roles, Missions, and Functions of the Armed Forces of the United States* (Washington, DC: Chairman of the Joint Chiefs of Staff, 1993), III-24; *Secretary of Defense Decisions: Roles, Missions, and Functions*, 14 April 1993, 2.

58. Discussions with Lieutenant General Wayne A. Downing on 26 April 1993 and with General Carl W. Stiner on 28 April 1993.

59. Roundtable discussions at USSOCOM Headquarters, AFSOC, and NAVSPECWARCOM, 27-30 April 1993; roundtables with SOF officers in the Pentagon, 20, 21, 23 April 1993.

60. Correspondence from the author to General Downing, 13 and 17 August 1993; from Col. Robert L. A. Lossius to author, 20 August 1993; memorandum from USSOCOM J5-0 to USSOCOM staff, "Proposal for USSOCOM 'Clearinghouse,'" 25 August 1993; correspondence from

author to Capt. Paul Shemella, USSOCOM J5-0, 1 October 1993 and to LtCol Rick Newton, USSOCOM J5-0), 28 October 1993; correspondence from General Downing to author, 4 January 1994. Those who wish to contribute ideas may write to: The SOF Clearinghouse, Hq USSOCOM/J5-0, 7701 Tampa Point Boulevard, MacDill AFB, FL 33621-5323.

VIII. Summary Assessments and Suggestions

Special Operations Forces were badly depleted before 1986, when congressional legislation created an Assistant Secretary of Defense for Special Operations and Low-Intensity Conflict, established a U.S. Special Operations Command, and directed the Secretary of Defense to devise a Major Force Program especially for SOF. Progress was slow at first, but soon gained momentum. Subsequent achievements have been impressive, but U.S. SOF cannot realize their full potential until senior U.S. national defense officials solve some significant residual problems.[1]

Impressive Accomplishments

Commendable accomplishments cover a broad spectrum of SOF activities:

- Established and organized ASD SO/LIC Office

- Established USSOCOM, its Army, Navy, and Air Force component commands

- Activated Special Forces, Civil Affairs/Psychological Operations, and Integration Commands within U.S. Army Special Operations Command

- Mobilized theater special operations commands and Theater Army Special Operations Support Commands

- Developed a counterterrorism joint task force that is a model for military and civilian counterparts worldwide

- Executed Command Arrangement Agreements with CINCs and Memoranda of Agreement with U.S. military services

- Developed a research, development, and acquisition system for SOF

- Formed intelligence architectures for USSOCOM, its component commands, and the five regionally oriented Commanders in Chief

- Formulated a planning, programming, and budgeting system for SOF

- Wrote a series of SOF doctrine manuals as authoritative guides

- Ensured special operations input to Defense Policy Guidance and routine participation in policy deliberations

- Refurbished and revitalized Special Operations Forces with new aircraft, Naval Special Warfare craft, high-tech weapons, equipment, and supplies

- Immensely improved SOF readiness, which sagged badly before 1986

- Particpated in every major U.S. military contingency operation since 1990 (Central Command employed more 9,000 SOF during Operation *Desert Storm*).

- Deployed more than 2,500 SOF personnel in over 40 countries on any given date. SOF are constantly on call for humanitarian assistance purposes, for which they are exceptionally well suited.

Residual Problems

Problems still exist. Several shortcomings previously discussed are connected herein with officials who seem best able to take corrective actions.

Consideration for the President

The National Security Council (NSC) has never effectively coordinated low-intensity conflict policies in consonance with a sense of Congress expressed in Section 1311, P.L. 99-661, 14 November 1986. The NSC has not disseminated guidance specifically designed to foster military special operations. A board for such purposes could prove invaluable in the post-Cold War World, if directed to guide, integrate, and otherwise focus all SO/LIC efforts of the U.S. Government.

Considerations for Congress

Some SOF problems beyond control by any official in the Executive Branch seem to merit consideration by Congress.   Topics concern congressional oversight, roles, missions, personnel management, and readiness.

- CINCSOC, component commanders, and other senior members of the U.S. military SOF community now lack institutional contacts on Capitol Hill where they can routinely keep Congress informed of plans, proposals, operations, and problems.   A Special Operations Panel or Subcommittee in each Armed Services Committee could provide useful forums for such purposes and simultaneously facilitate congressional oversight.

- Special operations alone seem ample to occupy the ASD SO/LIC full time, but *Title 10, U.S. Code,* imposes low-intensity conflict responsibilities on top of that work load.   Impartial investigators perhaps should review SO and LIC roles, which are related in some respects but nevertheless distinct, to determine whether continued amalgamation is advisable.

- Humanitarian assistance and theater search and rescue (TSAR) are SOF "activities" (missions), according to Section 167(j) of *Title 10, U.S. Code,* "insofar as [each] relates to special operations." Theater Commanders in Chief, who interpret that undefined qualifier very loosely, routinely call for SOF, who possess unparalleled capabilities but are so few that overcommitment sometimes results. At least four options are open: Revise *Title 10* so it explicitly defines the phrase "insofar as [each] relates to special operations;" relieve SOF of humanitarian and TSAR responsibilities; replace TSAR with combat search and rescue (CSAR) missions requiring clandestine infiltration/exfiltration capabilities; or augment active SOF that perform search and rescue functions.

- Section 403 (d)(5), *Title 50, U.S. Code*, directs the Central Intelligence Agency to "perform such other functions...as the National Security Council may from time to time direct." That citation has long justified CIA's jurisdiction over U.S. paramilitary operations. A review to determine whether USSOCOM should become the lead agency for paramilitary matters might prove useful.

- The Army lieutenant general who commands USASOC occupies the only three-star billet within the U.S. special operations community. Navy and Air Force flag officers, whose opportunities for promotion terminate at two stars, can aspire to assignment as CINCSOC only if parent services put them into a three-star conventional space. That never happens in the Navy and seldom in USAF. The two SEALs who enjoy flag rank never can serve on the Joint Staff or command a theater SOC, because they must always fill two SEAL slots within USSOCOM. Legislation that authorized a three-star Deputy CINCSOC and permanently allocated one star to every theater SOC would enhance the professional development of SOF flag officers and expand the pool of candidates who are well qualified to become CINCSOC.

- CINCSOC, his component commanders, regionally oriented CINCs, theater SOC Commanders, and their staffs all believe an undesirable imbalance exists between active and reserve component (AC/RC) civil affairs and PSYOP forces. Continued reliance on RC volunteers might be budgetarily advantageous but has practical drawbacks. Active duty personnel risk burnout, possibly followed by mission failure. Any one of three actions could significantly improve civil affairs and PSYOP postures (some combination would be even more beneficial): Alter the AC/RC mix in favor of active duty forces; authorize the National

Command Authorities to activate reserve civil affairs units that total up to 25,000 personnel, as General Stiner recently recommended in his *End of Tour Report* (appendix B); or establish an Individual Ready Reserve for civil affairs and PSYOP.

- Critics contend that USSOCOM has embraced research, development, and acquisition (RDA) procedures much like those that U.S. military services use to fill conventional force requirements. RDA cycles as a result often are too sluggish to satisfy relatively modest, but nevertheless imperative, needs for SOF-peculiar weapons, equipment, and supplies. Legislation that permits some relaxation of existing research, development, and acquisition regulations could make USSOCOM's system more responsive.

Considerations for Secretary of Defense

The Secretary of Defense is better able to solve some SOF problems than any other official in the Executive Branch. Each of the following issues has broad implications:

- No ASD SO/LIC as yet has been a special operations practitioner before appointment. The first nominee confirmed by Congress had direct access to the Secretary of Defense, for whom the ASD is the principal staff assistant and civilian adviser. Successors have reported to the Under Secretary of Defense for Policy. U.S. SOF and the conventional forces they complement both might benefit if each ASD SO/LIC henceforth possessed solid special operations credentials on confirmation day and met regularly with the Secretary of Defense to discuss SOF plans, programs, proposals, and problems that could significantly affect current and future U.S. military capabilities.

- The U.S. Air Force has done little to develop and retain professional SOF officers. AFSOC did not emerge until May 1990, 3 years after USSOCOM was activated. USAF still furnishes few seasoned SOF officers for key command and staff positions in USSOCOM Headquarters and at AFSOC. Every Air Force Major Command except AFSOC rates at least three stars.

USAF personnel management practices discourage Air Force special operations officers below flag rank. Helicopter crews feel especially slighted. Specific instructions to the Secretary of the Air Force and USAF Chief of Staff could terminate such practices.

■ The finest Special Operations Forces imaginable would be impotent without long-haul airlift able to deliver them wherever needed in time to accomplish assigned missions. There is no certainty, however, that Air Force Mobility Command's aging fleet, which serves many purposes, will be able to meet SOF's relatively modest needs indefinitely. Senior officers in USSOCOM Headquarters, at every component command, and in every U.S. military service express concern. Actions that expedite replacements for C-141 transports accordingly may be just as important as any SOF-specific program now in progress.

Considerations for ASD SO/LIC

The Assistant Secretary of Defense for Special Operations and Low-Intensity Conflict still lacks the influence that sponsors originally intended. Insufficient backing by the Secretary of Defense, already described, has been one basic inhibitor. The inexperience of congressionally confirmed incumbents has been another. A legally established Special Operations Policy Advisory Group (SOPAG), composed of SO/LIC experts and retirees who know how DoD operates, stands ready to assist the ASD SO/LIC and staff, but sessions in the past have often been disappointing. Future occupants of the ASD's Office might use the SOPAG to greater advantage if they presented one pressing problem at a time, then convened the group to debate respective opinions. Advice concerning resources for Special Mission Units, promotion opportunities for SOF flag officers, and wartime manning levels for theater special operations commands typify fundamental issues that SOPAG members seem ideally suited to address.

Considerations for Chairman, Joint Chiefs of Staff

The Chairman of the Joint Chiefs of Staff (CJCS) has quietly furnished strong behind-the-scenes support for CINCSOC and continues to develop special operations doctrine that encourages closer connections between SOF and conventional forces. CJCS might consider some additional actions:

- Act as a proponent of Special Operations Forces to encourage acceptance by senior officers in all U.S. military services.

- Review SOF missions, with particular attention to humanitarian assistance, search and rescue, narco conflict, security assistance, and paramilitary responsibilities, then advise the Secretary of Defense if adjustments seem advisable.

- Update *Joint Pub 0-2: Unified Action Armed Forces (UNAAF)* to reflect doctrinal changes contained in *Joint Pub 3-05: Doctrine for Joint Special Operations* and other documents in the *Pub 3* series.

- Recommend that the Secretary of Defense likewise amend *DoD Directive 5100.1: Functions of the Department of Defense and Its Major Components* to apportion SOF functions more specifically.

- Direct military schools/colleges to restructure curricula so that future U.S. commanders and their staffs more accurately appreciate the capabilities and limitations of Special Operations Forces.

- Review foreign language training requirements pursuant to military education responsibilities that Section 141(d)(1), *Title 10* prescribes and reset priorities if appropriate.

Considerations for CINCSOC

Personnel management and logistical support problems continue to afflict USSOCOM. Some are partly or entirely beyond CINCSOC's control, as previously noted, but others seem susceptible to his influence.

- Officers with little or no special operations experience continue to occupy key command and staff positions within USSOCOM Headquarters and AFSOC. CINCSOC could refuse to accept unqualified designees and instruct component commanders to do likewise. CINCSOC could then inform the Secretary of Defense if results remain unsatisfactory.

- Every theater special operations command currently depends extensively on Reserve Component augmentation packets for major exercises and emergencies. All SOCs are waiting for USSOCOM to complete the formation of two Battle Staffs (one primary, one alternate) that could reinforce SOC headquarters faster and more effectively. Both staffs currently are manned but lack essential weapons. Intensified efforts by CINCSOC to outfit Battle Staffs at the earliest possible date would ease the anxieties of SOC Commanders.

- USSOCOM has concluded Memoranda of Agreement (MOA) with the Army, Navy, and Air Force to codify respective responsibilities concerning planning, programming, budgeting, the execution of Major Force Program 11, and other support. Whether the USSOCOM-Navy MOA should serve as a model merits investigation.

Considerations for Theater CINCs

Senior officials in the U.S. special operations community believe that USSOCOM's lone civil affairs battalion is overworked. Many express similar views about SOC staffs, SOF helicopter crews, SEAL platoons, PSYOP, and selected Army Special Forces. Theater Commanders in Chief, who employ most Special Operations Forces that USSOCOM organizes, equips, trains, and provides, might use shorthanded SOF less liberally if they interpreted "requirements" as *Title 10* intends. Humanitarian and search/rescue missions then would call for SOF only "insofar as [each] pertains to special operations."

Prognosis

The Honorable John O. Marsh, Jr., when he was Secretary of the Army and soon to serve simultaneously as Acting ASD SO/LIC, opined that "failure in the past to link special operations with national strategy through the Defense Guidance—and thereby to develop doctrine—has prevented special operations...from gaining permanence and acceptability within the ranks of the military."[2] That deficiency has been corrected. Institutional changes are essentially complete, but military "cultures" are changing more slowly. Mutual distrust and misunderstandings still separate conventional forces from SOF, because not many of the former fully understand SOF capabilities and limitations. Too few special operations specialists have enough Pentagon experience to make "The System" work for them instead of against them. SOF constituencies on Capitol Hill, among U.S. military services, and in industry remain scant and tenuous; consequently, appropriate acceptance of Special Operations Forces will come only after all parties concerned complete a learning process and put doctrine into practices.

Notes

1. General Carl W. Stiner assesses accomplishments and shortcomings from CINCSOC's perspective in *End of Tour Report*, annex B.

2. John O. Marsh, Jr., "Keynote Address," in *Special Operations in U.S. Strategy*, eds. Frank R. Barnett, B. Hugh Trovar, and Richard H. Shultz (Washington, DC: National Defense University Press, 1984), 19.

Appendix A
Request from Senators Nunn and Cohen

REQUEST FROM SENATORS NUNN AND COHEN

SAM NUNN, GEORGIA, CHAIRMAN

J. JAMES EXON, NEBRASKA   STROM THURMOND, SOUTH CAROLINA
CARL LEVIN, MICHIGAN   JOHN W. WARNER, VIRGINIA
EDWARD M. KENNEDY, MASSACHUSETTS   WILLIAM S. COHEN, MAINE
JEFF BINGAMAN, NEW MEXICO   JOHN McCAIN, ARIZONA
JOHN GLENN, OHIO   TRENT LOTT, MISSISSIPPI
RICHARD C. SHELBY, ALABAMA   DAN COATS, INDIANA
ROBERT C. BYRD, WEST VIRGINIA   BOB SMITH, NEW HAMPSHIRE
BOB GRAHAM, FLORIDA   DIRK KEMPTHORNE, IDAHO
CHARLES S. ROBB, VIRGINIA   LAUCH FAIRCLOTH, NORTH CAROLINA
JOSEPH I. LIEBERMAN, CONNECTICUT

ARNOLD L. PUNARO, STAFF DIRECTOR
ANTHONY J. PRINCIPI, STAFF DIRECTOR FOR THE MINORITY

United States Senate

COMMITTEE ON ARMED SERVICES

WASHINGTON, DC 20510–6050

April 16, 1993

Mr. Joseph E. Ross
Director
Congressional Research Service
Library of Congress
Washington, D.C. 20540

Dear Mr. Ross:

We are writing to ask the Congressional Research Service to prepare a study of U.S. special operations forces. In particular, we would greatly appreciate John Collins, your Senior Specialist in National Defense, taking responsibility for this study.

In 1986, Congress passed legislation that established a new unified combatant command, the U.S. Special Operations Command, and the Department of Defense position of Assistant Secretary of Defense for Special Operations and Low Intensity Conflict. Seven years later, it would be helpful for the Congressional Research Service to assess the current and future capabilities of U.S. special operations forces.

We would like Mr. Collins to examine the personnel, equipment, and budgetary requirements of special operations forces. We hope that Mr. Collins' study will help us to understand these requirements in the post-Cold War world.

We authorize Mr. Collins to identify us as his sponsors and to discuss this project with any appropriate officials. Thank you for your consideration of this request.

Sincerely,

Sam Nunn

William S. Cohen

Appendix B
General Carl W. Stiner's End of Tour Report

GENERAL CARL W. STINER'S END OF TOUR REPORT

UNITED STATES SPECIAL OPERATIONS COMMAND
OFFICE OF THE COMMANDER IN CHIEF
MACDILL AIR FORCE BASE, FLORIDA 33608-6001

17 May 1993

MEMORANDUM FOR: Chairman of the Joint Chiefs of Staff

SUBJECT: End of Tour Report

1. As you well know, in June of 1990, I became the second Commander in Chief of the United States Special Operations Command. My predecessor, General Jim Lindsay, had done a masterful job of initially pulling together the special operations components from the three Services, staffing and training the joint headquarters, establishing appropriate management and oversight systems, and charting a course for the command's future. My challenge was to build on that start, mature the command, continue to revitalize our nation's special operations forces (SOF), and to employ SOF most fully and beneficially in support of the theater CINCs and our National Military Strategy.

2. My watch has been indeed interesting, challenging, and rewarding. With the support of the Services, the Joint Staff, the Office of the Secretary of Defense, and the Congress, we have maintained the momentum while meeting the challenge posed by the recently changed national and international political military environments. At a time when conventional threats and conventional forces are declining, the demands for SOF are increasing.

3. Although the command is, for the most part, healthy and moving in the right direction, there still remain much work to be done and many challenges, but likewise opportunities, for the future. I have highlighted in the attachment the most significant accomplishments, pertinent issues, and key recommendations for the future.

4. I thank you for your support and protection of SOF, and your visionary use of SOF in meeting the challenges of the new world order. I also thank you for your support of me; it could not have been better. It has been both a pleasure and privilege to serve my last assignment as the Commander in Chief of the United States Special Operations Command in the confidence and support of such an outstanding and professionally competent chain of command.

CARL W. STINER
General, U.S. Army
Commander in Chief

Atch
End of Tour Report

153

END OF TOUR REPORT

1. Overall Assessment:

    a. Overall, I believe that the United States Special Operations Command (USSOCOM) is in excellent shape. We have the finest special operations forces (SOF) that this nation has ever had. There is no armed forces in the world that can come close to our capability and our means to project and employ them.

    b. We have made great strides in the past six years since the formation of the command. We are capable of accomplishing all of the assigned missions given to us by Congress. We have instituted a joint training program which has significantly enhanced our readiness. This program includes a standardized management system and METLs for all subordinate units down to the squadron, company and team level. The command relationships with all of our subordinate elements (except the National Guard, addressed further on) have been solidified in command arrangement agreements, and are working correctly.

    c. Our relationships with the theater CINCs are superb. The cooperation between SOF and the theater CINCs is at an all time high, resulting in a significant increase in SOF employment by the theater CINCs. We continue to work closely with the theater CINCs on regional plans for the effective utilization of SOF in furthering regional and national security objectives.

    d. The command has stood up or assisted in improving several organizations that have contributed significantly to the smoothly functioning command and control of forward deployed SOF, to include the theater CINCs' Special Operations Commands (SOCs), the Theater Army Special Operations Support Commands (TASOSCs), and the Special Operations Command and Control Elements (SOCCEs) with Army Corps.

2. **Congressionally Mandated Agreements:** USSOCOM has completed all agreements with other Department of Defense (DOD) organizations to help carry out the mandates prescribed by Title 10, United States Code, Section 167. The most significant agreements include Command Arrangements Agreements (CAAs) with the Theater Commanders in Chief and Memoranda of Agreements (MOAs) with the Services. Executive Agreements concerning Major Force Program 11 (MFP-11); Training and Doctrine; Research, Development, & Acquisition; Military Construction; and Professional Development are now in place to establish the responsibilities and relationships between USSOCOM and other DOD organizations in regards to SOF. Today the total number of agreements signed exceeds 122, with additional ones in development.

3. **Personnel:**

a. The Services have provided SOF with adequate numbers of high-quality volunteers who have demonstrated the maturity, intelligence, skill, and physical toughness to complete the extensive and rigorous selection and training process. The generally higher-than-average selection/promotion rates for SOF personnel attest to their high quality throughout the full range of grades and specialties. Within the past 36 months, we have institutionalized processes to formally monitor promotion, retention, assignments, and professional military education (PME) of SOF personnel to ensure that we maintain the quality standards.

b. We continue to experience shortages in some grades and specialties, particularly in: Army Special Forces, Civil Affairs (CA), and Psychological Operations (PSYOP) company grade officers; Army Special Forces medics; and Navy SEAL Lieutenant Commanders and Commanders. We are working with the Services to resolve these shortfalls, but I would caution that we will have serious problems in the future if we cannot fix these shortages. The fast drawdown and the unknowns related to SERBs and RIFs, coupled with incentives to get out, are exacerbating the problem. Special management attention must be given to CA and PSYOP officers or we will end up with not enough for mission accomplishment.

c. We have recently created a joint SOF pre-command course to better prepare prospective SOF unit commanders and senior NCO leaders for their future responsibilities in the joint environment. Another major step forward in professional development is the establishment of a graduate-level curriculum of instruction in Special Operations/Low Intensity Conflict at the Naval Postgraduate School to better educate the future leadership of SOF.

4. **Intelligence:**

a. Intelligence readiness has been greatly advanced during the past three years. We have made major improvements in receipt, analysis and, most importantly, the dissemination of intelligence within the command and strengthened our intelligence relationships with the national intelligence agencies and the other CINCs. We have developed detailed plans called "intelligence architectures" for the five theater CINCs and for our components. In this analysis, we identified shortfalls that have now become new requirements in USSOCOM's intelligence programs. Our most successful program, SOCRATES, was the major intelligence data handling system for DESERT SHIELD/DESERT STORM and is in worldwide use today. SOCRATES is another example of how our rapid prototyping and budget authority can ·be used to enhance conventional as well as unconventional requirements.

b. We have improved intelligence support to the theater special operations commands, published SOF joint intelligence doctrine, and created a Joint Special Operations Intelligence Course at the Defense Intelligence College.

c. Lastly, we are fielding a new family of small, lightweight, and robust intelligence systems that will improve both jointness and interoperability which will be a major step forward in readiness. Work still remaining to be done includes the standing up of a Joint Intelligence Center and the further funding of new equipment such as the SOF intelligence vehicle and multi-mission advanced tactical terminal.

5. **Operations:**

a. USSOCOM deployed 10,000 special operations personnel in support of Operations DESERT SHIELD/DESERT STORM. SOF conducted all of their primary missions during these two operations, as well as the collateral missions of combat search and rescue and coalition warfare.

b. During the past three years USSOCOM has deployed forces to support all major contingency operations, to include Operations FIERY VIGIL, SEA ANGEL, PROVIDE COMFORT I & II, GTMO, PROVIDE PROMISE, PROVIDE HOPE, EASTERN EXIT, RESTORE HOPE, PROVIDE RELIEF, SHARP EDGE, and many classified activities.

c. Over the past year the command has averaged, on a weekly basis, over 2,600 personnel deployed, in 40+ countries, and 15 states, supporting U.S. national security policies. These numbers represent a 35 percent growth in the demand for SOF over previous years; we expect the growth trend to continue for the foreseeable future as additional emphasis is placed on peacetime engagement and nation assistance operations.

d. Forward basing is critical to SOF's ability to support the theater CINCs' peacetime and wartime mission requirements. SOF are uniquely trained to support forward presence operations through a variety of peacetime missions and provide an important initial contingency response capability. As we draw down conventional forces and close bases, we must maintain SOF's ability to provide this support. In December 1992, I sent personal messages to each of the theater CINCs requesting their support for the continued basing of current or enhanced SOF force structure in the AORs. Feedback from the theater CINCs unanimously indicates strong recognition of SOF's key role in support of theater CINC's peacetime and wartime missions.

6. **Logistics:**

a. Operation DESERT SHIELD/DESERT STORM demonstrated that while the Services could provide common types of support to Army and Air Force SOF, and to SEALS when they were afloat, SOF-peculiar support was deficient. USSOCOM, with support from the Services, developed a number of fixes to include providing better management and funding of SOF war reserve materiel, creation of operational contingency stocks, upgrading and fleshing out the capabilities of the special operations support battalion, and creation of a SOF "mini-depot" to provide responsive, cost-effective repair or modification for critical equipment and stockage of a small amount of highly specialized equipment for contingency operations.

b. SOF must continue to receive adequate "service-common" logistical support while developing innovative and cost-effective ways to obtain SOF-peculiar support.

7. **Doctrine:**

a. We have made great strides in this critical area. A few years ago joint SOF doctrine was practically nonexistent. Today joint SOF doctrine has been published in keystone manuals, which range from topical coverage of SOF roles, missions, and functions to specific joint SOF tactics, techniques, and procedures.

b. Equally as important, SOF doctrine has been integrated into appropriate Service doctrinal publications and has been fully integrated into most Service school instruction, although there is still much more to be accomplished in Service schools.

8. **Force Structure:**

a. Over the past three years we have been able to program some badly needed Active component structure growth. We have added a Special Forces Group and will soon increase the number of SEAL teams and Air Force Special Operations Squadrons while boosting the strengths of the heavily committed CA and PSYOP units. We also plan to add an austere, multi-service aviation Foreign Internal Defense organization to respond to the needs of several of the theater CINCs for assisting developing countries to more effectively utilize and employ aviation assets in support of ground operations.

b. I must point out that we are still in critical need of additional Active component CA and PSYOP units; there are simply not enough of these units to meet today's commitments. We must also strike a better balance between Active and Reserve component SOF units. Reserve units, particularly CA, which are no longer needed must be inactivated.

c. The designation of CA and PSYOP units as SOF was a major milestone and will enable USSOCOM to clear up some of the legal ambiguities and institutional misunderstandings that have existed in the past and will allow us to better utilize their unique capabilities at home and abroad.

d. We have stood up the theater Special Operations Commands (SOCs) and clearly codified their roles and missions as a sub-unified command of the theater CINCs. In FY 93, USSOCOM assumed responsibility for planning and programming SOC requirements. Four of the five SOCs are now authorized brigadier generals as commanders, and as the Atlantic Command expands its joint service training role for joint CONUS forces, I foresee the need to upgrade SOCLANT to a brigadier general position to handle the increased responsibility, as SOCLANT takes over many SOF staff areas of responsibility now handled by the CINCLANT staff. We stood up the SOCs with bare minimum staffing. As their utility has been recognized, and as the overall utility of SOF deployments in theaters has risen, we must ensure that the SOCs are manned at a level commensurate with their increasing responsibilities.

e. Similarly, the Theater Army Special Operations Support Commands (TASOSCs) were stood up with very small staffs. A study on the TASOSCs was completed in May 1992. It was forwarded to Congress in response to congressional language in the FY 92 Joint Appropriations Conference Report directing the elimination of the TASOSCs from the SOF force structure. The TASOSC study findings were briefed to congressional staffers and resulted in congressional language in the FY 93 Joint Appropriations Conference Report that retained the TASOSCs. As we clarify the roles and missions of the TASOSCs, as the utility of this organization in supporting the increasing number of SOF peacetime deployments is demonstrated, and as the essential role of the TASOSC supporting Operations DESERT SHIELD/DESERT STORM is recognized, these commands, too, will need to be resourced in accordance with their increasing roles.

9. **Communications:** We have improved the overall SOF communications readiness since August 1990 when SOF first deployed in support of Operation DESERT SHIELD. The command's focus has been on team level communications ranging from small inter-team radios to lightweight UHF SATCOM terminals. Communications readiness has been improved by various means: through the expenditure of MFP-11 funds for NDI systems, through coordination with the Services for priority fielding of "common items" to SOF units, and through accelerated development efforts for SOF-peculiar systems. In short, C4 readiness is at an acceptable level across the force and team level modernization will be complete by the end of FY 94.

10. Program and Budget:

a. The need for SOF is increasing in an emerging non-traditional, multi-polar world. Despite increasing demand by theater CINCs, and SOF's expanding missions, proportionate reimbursement in Operations and Maintenance (O&M) funding has not materialized. In FY 91, USSOCOM received compensation for Operations DESERT SHIELD/DESERT STORM and other unbudgeted operations. During FY 92, unprogrammed, unbudgeted operations increased 35 percent, and FY 93 rates already exceed those. Lack of reimbursement is forcing USSOCOM to mortgage the future for current operational requirements. For FY 93, a predicted $25 million O&M shortfall required restructuring and delay of several acquisition programs. Continued restructuring will put these programs at risk and SOF will be inadequately equipped for the capabilities needed for the future. PBD 191's $36 million RDT&E decrement and proposed funding for the former Soviet Union threat reduction (Nunn-Lugar) exacerbates the problem.

b. As the Head of a Defense Agency, USCINCSOC deals financially with OSD as a Service equivalent. To ensure issues such as the "additive end strength" nature of SOF and common equipment support continue, close coordination with the Services and OSD is necessary. Inclusion of the USSOCOM Director of Resources in the monthly MIL-5 meetings could strengthen the cooperation among USSOCOM, the Services, and OSD.

11. Special Operations Research, Development, and Acquisition:

a. During FY 92, I appointed Mr. Gary L. Smith as the Special Operations Acquisition Executive and Senior Procurement Executive and delegated Head of Agency authority to him. We concurrently updated all internal acquisition policies and renegotiated new umbrella RDT&E memorandums of agreement (MOA) and several program specific MOAs with the Services. As a result, we have improved our acquisition management and have more clearly defined lines of authority, accountability, and responsibility of SOF-peculiar weapons systems and equipment.

b. On 2 March 1993, I signed an Acquisition Decision Memorandum authorizing an Acquisition Category III (ACAT III) program for a combatant craft, the MARK V Special Operations Craft, to enter Concept Exploration and Definition (Acquisition Phase 0). We have decided to retain program management control and milestone decision authority for this program. The MARK V program represents the first significant program to be executed completely by USSOCOM's Special Operations Research, Development, and Acquisition Center (SORDAC) and was a major step forward for the command.

c.   During Operations DESERT SHIELD/DESERT STORM, USSOCOM, using our unique authority for SOF-peculiar acquisition, responded to urgent needs and validated 23 of 24 USCENTCOM requested items, procured 19 of the items, and had them in the hands of SOF troops in theater, with appropriate new equipment training conducted, within 30 days.   These actions demonstrated the utility of such needed acquisition authorities.

d.   SORDAC was reorganized in FY 93 to provide abbreviated lines of responsibilities and authority, and to improve accountability for acquisition management functions within Headquarters, USSOCOM. This objective was accomplished by aligning similar acquisition programs under the control of a Program Executive Officer (PEO), with the PEO reporting directly to the Special Operations Acquisition Executive (SOAE).   This reorganization was the final step toward establishing a system for USSOCOM to better manage all investment programs.

12. **Modernization:** The following are ongoing major modernization actions that are essential to the capability of SOF for meeting the needs of the future.

a.   Aerial Mobility.

(1)   Army special operations aviation is currently fielding the most advanced penetrator helicopters in the world, the MH-60K (23 each) and the MH-47E (26 each). They will provide increased medium-range capability for low-level flight in adverse weather and precision navigation through unfamiliar, mountainous terrain. These helicopters are equipped with extended range fuel systems, aerial refueling capability, forward-looking infrared (FLIR) systems, and upgraded engines. Coupled with the upgraded MH-53Js, these helicopters will provide a superb capability for short- and medium-range penetration.   However, helicopter technology has reached its limits for inserting SOF over extended distances into denied areas and exfiltrating them in one night. We need a greater capability, which means another platform.

(2)   The 24 MC-130H Combat Talon II aircraft will dramatically improve our long-range capability to employ SOF. The aircraft is capable of low-level, night, adverse weather penetration of hostile air space to infiltrate or resupply SOF. Twelve have already been fielded, and fielding of the remaining twelve should be complete by the end of FY 94.

b. Maritime Mobility.

(1)   SDV platoon readiness will be enhanced by modernizing the SEAL Delivery Vehicles (SDV) and swimmer life support systems to increase short-range missions capacity. Fielding the Advanced Swimmer Delivery System (ASDS) (6 each) in the later part of the decade will provide significant improvements over current capabilities. The ASDS will provide increased range and speed, and will protect SEALs from extreme cold water conditions, resulting in improved performance at the target. It will also enhance the survivability of the delivery system's host ship. The ASDS will give SOF covert capabilities never before available. These two programs will enhance maritime infiltration and exfiltration.

(2) The USS CYCLONE Class Patrol, Coastal (PC) (13 each) and the air transportable MK V patrol boat (16 each) will modernize Navy special operations direct action, special reconnaissance and coastal patrol and interdiction capabilities. The mission of the PC is coastal patrol and interdiction, with a secondary mission of SEAL support. The MK V patrol boat's mission is medium-range insertion and extraction of SOF in a low- to medium-threat environment. The system combines a high performance, highly versatile, reliable, and rugged combatant craft with a transporter. The entire system will be air transportable, allowing rapid response to developing situations around the world.

c. The development of the Joint Advanced Special Operations Radio System (JASORS) is USSOCOM's most important C3I modernization program. When fielded this radio will replace several older, heavier, and less reliable radios with a single system that will greatly increase SOF's ability to communicate within SOF and also with conventional forces. It offers a secure, low probability of interception and detection capability to improve the survivability of SOF teams operating in denied areas. JASORS will be interoperable with communications systems used by conventional forces as well as theater CINC C3I systems.

d. The AC-130U gunship (13 each) will greatly enhance AFSOC's capability to support SOF and conventional forces in contingency operations. The AC-130U will be the best gunship in the world in terms of navigation, target acquisition, adverse weather capabilities, and accuracy and lethality of fires. An additional benefit of the gunship is its greater stand-off capability and its ability to minimize collateral damage with pinpoint firing accuracy.

e.   The Special Operations Medical Training Center, a new facility to be built at Fort Bragg, will significantly improve the training and sustainment of a key element of SOF utility.   The benefits of this facility will be twofold.   First, it will enhance SOF medical training significantly by tailoring courses for specific needs with a regional orientation, and by training all SOF medics to the same standard.   Second, it will save significant amounts of money in reduced TDY costs.   We expect the facility to pay for itself in only five years based on TDY savings.

13.   **Issues:**

a.   25K Reserve Call Up: The increasing demand for civil affairs units to support theater CINCs has severely strained the ability of the Army's only active duty CA battalion to meet all the requirements and still maintain a reasonable OPTEMPO for its personnel.   The activation of the second active CA battalion will partially relieve this shortfall.   But the long term solution, one that will guarantee adequate CA units, and other SOF units, to meet future increasing demands, is for passage of legislation that will authorize the National Command Authorities to activate up to 25,000 Reserve component personnel without Congressional approval.   The call up of units is necessary;   individual volunteers are of little value.

b.   Command and Control of National Guard Units: The only remaining gap between USSOCOM's legislated mission of providing trained and ready SOF to theater CINCs, and the ability of this command to monitor and ensure that readiness, lies with National Guard units.   USSOCOM has not been assigned all of the National Guard forces that are SOF, specifically Air National Guard units. Assignment of these units to USSOCOM is essential if we are to meet our mandated missions and legislated responsibilities for readiness.   The Air National Guard units are critical SOF units that, in the case of the COMMANDO SOLO aircraft, contain capabilities found only in that unit and not in the active force.

c.   Shortfalls in Major Procurement Accounts: When USSOCOM took over several major equipment procurement programs from the Services, the programs had significant shortfalls in money due to cost overruns. Each program represents a critical component of SOF modernization and future capabilities that will be essential if SOF are to continue to contribute to national security without undue risk to operators and mission accomplishment.   If we are not allocated the money to fix these programs they will be in jeopardy.

d. AC/RC Mix: Much of the Reserve component force structure for SOF was created in response to the Cold War. While the active force structure was always regional in character, and designed to support both wartime and peacetime low intensity conflicts, much of the RC force structure was designed to support a global war with the Soviet Union or a major theater wide war in Europe. With the dissolution of the Soviet Union and the severe reduction in the immediate threat of a global or theater wide war, the United States no longer needs many of the RC units that were put into the force structure specifically for this mission. This is particularly true of RC civil affairs units. If we do not remove these units from the force structure we will be paying badly needed defense dollars for unneeded force structure, at the expense of other, vital programs.

Appendix C
Glossary

Active Components: U.S. Army, Navy, Air Force, and Marine Corps organizations that perform all duties in Federal service. Reserve Component forces on active duty are excluded. *See also* Reserve Components.

additive end strength: CINCSOC pays for SOF manpower with Major Force Program-11 funds. Each parent service, however, must add to its authorized conventional personnel strength any (Army, Navy, or Air Force) increase in Special Operations Forces since 1 December 1989. Each service also may subtract any decrease in SOF personnel since that date.

administrative control: Direction or exercise of authority over subordinate or other organizations with respect to administrative matters such as personnel management, supply, services, and other activities not included in the operational missions of subordinate or other organizations.

Air Force special operations detachment: A squadron-size headquarters which could control different types of SOF aircraft. It is normally subordinate to an Air Force SOC, JSOTF, or Joint Task Force, depending upon size and duration of the operation. Also called AFSOD.

Air Force Special Operations Forces: Those Active and Reserve Component Air Force forces designated by the Secretary of Defense that are specifically organized, trained, and equipped to conduct and support special operations. Also called AFS.

antiterrorism: Defensive measures used to reduce the vulnerability of individuals and property to terrorism. *See also* counterterrorism; terrorism.

architecture: A framework or structure that portrays relationships among all the elements of the subject force, system, or activity.

area of responsibility: A specific geographic plot within which superiors authorize a military commander to operate. Coordination is required whenever neighboring commanders deploy forces in close proximity or cross designated boundaries.

area oriented: Personnel or units whose organization, mission, training, and equipment are based on projected operational deployment to a specific geographic or demographic region.

Army Special Operations Forces: Active and reserve component Army forces designated by the Secretary of Defense that are specifically organized, trained, and equipped to conduct and support special operations. Also called ARSOF.

assigned forces: Personnel and/or units that are permanent parts of a parent organization whose commander commands, controls, and administers them, except when they are temporarily detached for specific purposes. *See also* attached forces.

attached forces: Personnel and/or units that are temporarily placed in an organization for specific purposes. The commander receiving attachments exercises command and control, subject to limitations imposed by attachment orders. The parent organization normally retains administrative responsibilities. *See also* assigned forces.

capability: The ability to execute specific courses of action against particular opposition at particular times and places.

civil affairs: Activities that establish, maintain, influence, or exploit relations between military forces, civil authorities (both governmental and nongovernmental), and the civilian populace in a friendly, neutral, or hostile area before, during, after, or in lieu of other military operations. Civil affairs may include performance by military forces of activities and functions that normally are the responsibility of local governments.

clandestine operations: Activities sponsored or conducted by governmental departments or agencies in such a way as to assure secrecy or concealment. They differ from covert operations in that emphasis is placed on concealment of the operation rather than on concealing the sponsor's identity. *See also* covert operations; low-visibility operations.

coalition force: An armed force of two or more nations who have formed a temporary alliance for some specific purpose. *See also* combined operations.

combatant command: *See* unified command.

combatant command authority: Non-transferable command responsibilities established by *Title 10, United States Code,* Section 164 and exercised only by Commanders in Chief of

U.S. unified commands. Directorship over all aspects of joint military training, operations, and logistics necessary to accomplish prescribed missions is included. *See also* command; operational control.

combat search and rescue: The use of aircraft, surface craft, submarines, and specialized teams to recover distressed personnel during wartime or contingency operations. Also called CSAR. *See also* search and rescue; theater search and rescue.

combatting terrorism: Actions taken to oppose terrorism throughout the entire threat spectrum. *See also* antiterrorism; counterterrorism.

combined operations: Military activities that involve armed forces from two or more nations. *See also* coalition force.

command: Lawful authority and responsibility to organize, administer, and employ assigned/attached forces in performance of designated duties during peacetime and war. *See also* combatant command authority; operational control.

compartmentation: Establishment and management of any military organization so that information about the personnel, organization, or activities of one component is made available to any other component only to the extent required for the performance of assigned duties. *See also* Special Mission Unit.

component commands: The principal subordinate commands of any U.S. unified command. *See also* unified command.

contingency: An event that political-military authorities reasonably anticipate might occur. Military commanders accordingly prepare plans and maintain armed forces for deterrent, offensive, and/or defensive purposes, and take actions if directed. *See also* crisis.

conventional forces, operations: Regular military organizations, hostilities, and hardware that exclude nuclear, chemical, and biological weapons. *See also* special operations; Special Operations Forces.

counterdrug: Active measures taken to detect, monitor, and counter the production, trafficking, and use of illegal drugs. Also called CD.

counterinsurgency: 1. Political, economic, social, military, and paramilitary measures that indigenous governments and associates use to forestall or defeat insurgencies. 2. Similar measures occupying powers use to forestall or defeat resistance movements. *See also* insurgency.

counterterrorism: Offensive measures designed to deter, and if necessary defeat, terrorism. *See also* antiterrorism; combatting terrorism; terrorism.

covert operations: Actions that are planned and executed so as to conceal the identity of, or permit plausible denial by, the sponsor. They differ from clandestine operations in that emphasis is placed on concealment of identity of sponsor rather than on concealment of the operation. *See also* clandestine operations: low-visibility operations.

crisis: An international emergency with adverse implications for observers as well as afflicted parties. Some crises are short, others are long. *See also* contingency; *in extremis.*

deception: Measures designed to mislead enemies by manipulation, distortion, or falsification of evidence and thereby induce them to react in a manner prejudicial to their interests.

denied area: An area under hostile control in which friendly forces cannot expect to operate successfully within existing operational constraints.

direct action: Short-duration strikes and other small-scale offensive activities conducted primarily by Special Operations Forces. Raids, ambushes, and hostage rescue operations are representative.

disaster relief: Humanitarian assistance in the United States or abroad to alleviate suffering caused by natural and manmade catastrophes such as fires, floods, earthquakes, and riots. *See also* humanitarian assistance.

evasion and escape: Procedures and operations whereby military personnel and other selected individuals are enabled to emerge from enemy-held or hostile territory to areas under friendly control.

exfiltration: The clandestine extraction of personnel or units from hostile or denied areas. *See also* infiltration.

expeditionary forces: Any U.S. military formation designed to operate outside the United States during peacetime or war.

foreign internal defense: Participation by civilian and military agencies of a government in programs another government undertakes to forestall or defeat insurgency, transnational terrorism, lawlessness, or subversion.

guerrilla warfare: Military and paramilitary operations conducted in enemy-held or hostile territory by irregular, predominantly indigenous forces.

humanitarian and civil assistance: Aid designed to improve the quality of life in a foreign country. Chapter 20, *Title 10* limits DoD contributions to medical, dental, and veterinary care provided in rural areas of a country; construction of rudimentary surface transportation systems; well drilling and construction of basic sanitation facilities; rudimentary construction and repair of public facilities; and transportation of relief supplies. DoD interprets the term more broadly. *See also* disaster relief.

in extremis: A situation of such exceptional urgency that immediate action must be taken to minimize imminent loss of life or catastrophic degradation of U.S. political or military posture. *See also* crisis.

infiltration: The clandestine insertion of personnel or units into hostile or denied areas. *See also* exfiltration.

insurgency: Extended, organized efforts by domestic groups to overthrow the established order (not necessarily a government), seize political power by subversive and coercive means, and sometimes (not always) alter social systems. *See also* counterinsurgency.

irregular forces: Armed individuals or groups who are not members of regular armed forces, police, or other internal security forces.

Joint Force Special Operations Component Commander: The commander within a unified command, subordinate unified command, or joint task force responsible to the establishing commander for making recommendations on the proper employment of Special Operations Forces and assets, planning and coordinating special operations, or accomplishing such operational missions as may be assigned. The Joint Force Special Operations Component Commander normally has the preponderance of Special Operations Forces and the requisite command and control capabilities. Also called JFSOCC.

joint special operations task force: A joint task force of special operations units from more than one Service. It may have conventional units assigned or attached to support the conduct of specific missions. Also called JSOTF. *See also* joint task force.

joint task force: An *ad hoc* organization that contains elements of two or more armed services, is established to accomplish limited objectives, and dissolves when its mission is complete. The Secretary of Defense, Commanders in Chief of U.S. combatant commands, and commanders of existing joint task forces have authority to form JTFs. *See also* standing joint task force.

low-intensity conflict: Political-military confrontation between contending states or groups below conventional war and above the routine, peaceful competition among states. It frequently involves protracted struggles of competing principles and ideologies. Low-intensity conflict ranges from subversion to the use of armed force. It is waged with political, economic, informational, and military instruments. Low-intensity conflicts are often localized, generally in the Third World, but may have regional and global security implications. Also called LIC.

Marine Expeditionary Unit: A reinforced Marine infantry battalion, reinforced helicopter squadron, and a service support group that are organized, trained, and equipped to conduct quick-reaction operations, specifically as a part of an Amphibious Ready Group. *See also* Marine Expeditionary Unit (Special Operations Capable).

Marine Expeditionary Unit (Special Operations Capable): A forward-deployed U.S. Marine Corps unit able to conduct limited special operations. It is not a Secretary of Defense designated Special Operations Force but, when directed by the National Command Authorities and/or the theater commander, may conduct hostage recovery or other special operations *in extremis*. Also called MEU (SOC). *See also* Marine Expeditionary Unit.

mission: A task that the President of the United States or Secretary of Defense assigns to a unified command. Tasks assigned to subordinate forces at every level.

National Command Authorities: The President of the United States and the Secretary of Defense or their duly deputized alternates or successors. Also called NCA.

Naval Special Warfare: Naval activities that usually are unorthodox and often are covert or clandestine. Activities include unconventional warfare, psychological operations, beach and coastal reconnaissance, operational deception, counterinsurgency, coastal and river interdiction, and certain special tactical intelligence collection operations. Also called NSW.

Naval Special Warfare Forces: Those Active and Reserve Component naval forces designated by the Secretary of Defense that are specifically organized, trained, and equipped to conduct and support special operations. Also called NAFSOV.

Naval Special Warfare group: Navy organizations to which most Naval Special Warfare forces are assigned for some operational and all administrative purposes. It consists of a group headquarters with command, control, communications, and support staff, SEAL teams, special boat squadrons, subordinate special boat units, and SEAL delivery vehicle teams. The group is the source of all deployed Naval Special Warfare forces and administratively supports Naval Special Warfare Units assigned to theater CINCs. The group staff provides general operational direction and coordinates the activities of its subordinate units. Also called NSWG.

Naval Special Warfare Special Operations Component: The Navy Special Operations Component of a unified or subordinate unified command or joint special operations task force. Also called NAVSOC.

Naval Special Warfare Unit: Permanently theater-deployed command element to control and support attached Naval Special Warfare forces. Also called NSWU.

operational control: Transferable command authority that may be exercised by commanders at any echelon at or below the level of combatant command. Operational control is inherent in combatant command and is the authority to organize and employ subordinate commands and forces, assign tasks, designate objectives, and issue directives necessary to accomplish missions. Operational control, which includes authoritative direction over all aspects of military operations and joint training, normally is exercised through service component commanders. Operational control does not include logistics, administration, discipline, internal organization, or unit training. Also called OPCON. *See also* combatant command authority.

paramilitary forces, operations: 1. Land, sea, and air forces of a nation which have a distinctive chain of command, primarily perform internal security functions beyond the ability of law enforcement units, and supplement the regular military establishment as required. 2. Guerrillas and other armed irregulars that use quasimilitary tactics and techniques.

pararescue team: Specially trained personnel qualified to penetrate to the site of an incident by land, sea, or parachute, render medical aid, and rescue survivors.

peacekeeping: Nonviolent efforts of a military force, interposed between belligerents by mutual consent, to maintain a truce or otherwise discourage hostilities. *See also* peacemaking.

peacemaking: Efforts by a military force to prevent armed conflict in a specified locale or terminate hostilities by force, if necessary. *See also* peacekeeping.

psychological operations: Planned operations that convey selected information and indicators to influence the emotions, motives, objective reasoning, and ultimately the behavior of foreign governments, organizations, groups, and individuals. The purpose of psychological operations is to induce or reinforce foreign attitudes and behavior favorable to the originator's objectives. Also called PSYOP.

Rangers: Rapidly deployable Army airborne light infantry organized and trained to conduct highly complex joint direct action operations in coordination with, or in support of, other special operations units of all services. Rangers can also execute direct action operations in support of conventional missions and can operate as conventional light infantry when properly augmented.

Reserve Components: Armed forces not in active service, specifically the U.S. Army National Guard and Army Reserve; the Naval Reserve; Marine Corps Reserve; Air National Guard and Air Force Reserve; and Coast Guard Reserve. *See also* Active Components.

sea-air-land team (SEAL): A group of officers and individuals specially trained and equipped to conduct unconventional and paramilitary operations and to train personnel of allied nations in such operations, including surveillance and reconnaissance in and from restricted waters, rivers, and coastal areas. Commonly referred to as a SEAL team.

search and rescue: The use of aircraft, surface craft, submarines, specialized teams, and equipment to search for and rescue personnel in distress on land or at sea. Also called SAR. *See also* combat search and rescue; theater search and rescue.

security assistance: Group of programs authorized by the Foreign Assistance Act of 1961, as amended, and the Arms Export Control Act of 1976, as amended, or other related statutes by which the United States provides defense articles, military training, and other defense-related services, by grant, loan, credit, or cash sales, in furtherance of national policies and objectives.

special activities: Activities conducted in support of national foreign policy objectives which are planned and executed so that the role of the U.S. Government is not apparent or acknowledged publicly. They are not intended to influence U.S. domestic political processes, public opinion, policies, or media and do not include diplomatic activities or the collection and production of intelligence or related support functions.

special boat unit: U.S. Navy forces organized, trained, and equipped to conduct or support naval special warfare, riverine warfare, coastal patrol and interdiction, and joint special operations with patrol boats or other combatant craft designed primarily for special operations. Also called SBU.

Special Forces: U.S. Army units organized, trained, and equipped specifically to conduct five primary missions: unconventional warfare, foreign internal defense, direct action, special reconnaissance, and counterterrorism. Also called SF and Green Berets.

Special Forces group: An Army combat arms organization that plans, conducts, and supports special operations activities in all operational environments in peace, during contingencies/crises, and war. It consists of a group headquarters and headquarters company, a support company, and Special Forces battalions. The group can operate as a single unit, but normally the battalions plan and conduct operations from widely separated locations. The group provides general operational direction and synchronizes the activities of subordinate battalions.

Special Mission Unit: An elite Special Operations Force organized, equipped, and trained for counterterrorism, direct action, strategic reconnaissance, and other missions that usually are compartmented and highly classified. Also called SMU. *See also* compartmentation.

special operations: Operations conducted by specially organized, trained, and equipped military and paramilitary forces to achieve military, political, economic, or psychological objectives by unconventional military means in hostile, denied, or politically sensitive areas. These operations are conducted during peacetime, contingencies/crises, and war, independently or in coordination with conventional forces. Political-military considerations frequently require clandestine, covert, or low visibility techniques and oversight at the national level. Special operations differ from conventional operations in degree of physical and political risk, operational techniques, modes of employment, independence from friendly support, and dependence on detailed operational intelligence and indigenous assets. Also so called SO. *See also* Special Operations Forces.

Special Operations Command: A joint command composed of designated Special Operations Forces that is established by a unified or other joint force commander to prepare for, plan, and execute special operations within the joint force commander's Area of Operations, or as directed by the National Command Authorities. Also called SOC.

Special Operations Forces: Military units of the Army, Navy, and Air Force which are organized, trained, and equipped specifically to conduct special operations. Also called SOF. *See also* special operations.

special operations peculiar: Equipment, materials, supplies, and services required for special operations and for which there is no broad conventional force requirement. The term often involves nondevelopmental or special category items that incorporate evolving technology. It may include stocks of obsolete weapons and equipment designed to support indigenous personnel who do not possess sophisticated operational capabilities.

special reconnaissance: *See* strategic (special) reconnaissance.

special tactics team: An Air Force unit composed primarily of special operations combat control and pararescue personnel. It supports joint special operations air/ground/maritime missions by selecting, surveying, and establishing assault zones; providing assault zone terminal guidance and air traffic control; conducting direct action and personnel recovery missions; providing medical care and evacuation; and coordinating, planning and conducting air, ground, and naval gunfire support operations.

standing joint task force: A permanent joint task force that is organized, equipped, and trained to undertake various missions whenever and wherever directed. *See also* joint task force.

strategic (special) reconnaissance: Operations to collect or verify information of national or theater-level significance concerning the capabilities, intentions, and activities of actual or potential enemies; geographic, demographic, and other characteristics of a particular area; and post-strike battle damage data.

subordinate unified command: A unified command within a unified command, established by the Commander in Chief of the parent organization. Normally includes two or more component commands. *See also* component commands; unified commands.

terrorism: Public, repetitive violence or threats of violence to achieve sociopolitical objectives by inspiring widespread fear among people not personally involved. Terrorists hope to disrupt community routines so severely that compliance with their demands eventually may seem preferable to further disorder. *See also* antiterrorism; counterterrorism.

theater search and rescue: Search and rescue operations conducted for regionally-oriented U.S. Commanders in Chief in peacetime, during contingencies/crises, and war. *See also* combat search and rescue; search and rescue.

unconventional warfare: Military and paramilitary operations conducted in enemy-held, enemy-controlled, or politically sensitive territory. Prominent aspects include guerrilla warfare, evasion and escape, subversion, sabotage, and other operations of a low visibility, covert, or clandestine nature. Unconventional warfare operations are prosecuted by predominantly indigenous personnel, usually supported and directed in varying degrees by outsiders during all conditions of war or peace. Also called UW.

unified command: A U.S. combatant command with geographic or functional responsibilities which includes forces from two or more military services. It has a broad, continuing mission and is established by the President, through the Secretary of Defense, with the advice and assistance of the Chairman of the Joint Chiefs of Staff. *See also* subordinate unified command.

Appendix D
Abbreviations and Acronyms

AC	active component
ADCON	administrative control
AFRES	Air Force Reserve
AFSOC	Air Force Special Operations Command
ANG	Air National Guard
AOR	area of responsibility
ARNG	Army National Guard
ASD	Assistant Secretary of Defense
Bde	brigade
Bn	battalion
C^3I	command, control, communications, and intelligence
CA	civil affairs
CAPOC	Civil Affairs and Psychological Operations Command
CENTCOM	Central Command
CINC	Commander in Chief
CINCSOC	Commander in Chief, U.S. Special Operations Command
CJCS	Chairman of the Joint Chiefs of Staff
COCOM	combatant command
Comd	command
CONUS	Continental United States
C/S	Chief of Staff
CSAR	combat search and rescue
CT	counterterrorism
CTJTF	counterterrorism joint task force
DA	direct action
Det	detachment
EUCOM	European Command
FID	foreign internal defense
Grp	group
HUMINT	human intelligence
IRR	Individual Ready Reserve

J-3	Joint Staff (Operations)
J-3 (SOD)	J-3 (Special Operations Division)
JSCP	Joint Strategic Capabilities Plan
JSOA	Joint Special Operations Agency
JSOC	Joint Special Operations Command
JSOTF	Joint Special Operations Task Force
LANTCOM	Atlantic Command
LIC	low-intensity conflict
MAC	Military Airlift Command
MEU	Marine Expeditionary Unit
MFP	major force program
MILPERS	military personnel
MOA	Memorandum of Agreement
NAVSPECWARCOM	Naval Special Warfare Command
NCA	National Command Authorities
NG	National Guard
NR	Naval Reserve
NSC	National Security Council
NSW	Naval Special Warfare
NSWG	Naval Special Warfare Group
NSWU	Naval Special Warfare Unit
O&M	operations and maintenance
OPCON	operational control
OSD	Office of the Secretary of Defense
PACOM	Pacific Command
P.L.	Public Law
POM	Program Objective Memorandum
PPBS	Planning, Programming, Budgeting System
PSYOP	psychological operations
RC	reserve component
RDA	research, development, and acquisition
SBU	special boat unit
SDV	SEAL delivery vehicle
SEAL	sea-air-land
SF	Special Forces
SMOTEC	Special Missions Operational Test and Evaluation Center
SMU	Special Missions Unit
SO	special operations
SOAR	Special Operations Aviation Regiment

SOC	Special Operations Command
SOCCENT	Special Operations Command, Central
SOCEUR	Special Operations Command, Europe
SOC-K	Special Operations Command, Korea
SOCLANT	Special Operations Command, Atlantic
SOCOM	Special Operations Command
SOCPAC	Special Operations Command, Pacific
SOCSOUTH	Special Operations Command, South
SOD	Special Operations Division
SOF	Special Operations Forces
SOPAG	Special Operations Policy Advisory Group
SOUTHCOM	Southern Command
SOW	Special Operations Wing
Sq	squadron
SR	strategic or special reconnaissance
TASOSC	Theater Army Special Operations Support Command
TSAR	theater search and rescue
USACAPOC	U.S. Army Civil Affairs and Psychological Operations Command
USAR	U.S. Army Reserve
USASFC	U.S. Army Special Forces Command
USASOC	U.S. Army Special Operations Command
USNR	U.S. Naval Reserve
USSOCOM	U.S. Special Operations Command
UW	unconventional warfare

Index

About the Author

John M. Collins has specialized in military matters for 52 years. He joined the U.S. Army as a private in 1942 and retired as a colonel in 1972 after wartime service in Europe, Korea, and Vietnam. He has been Senior Specialist in National Defense at the Library of Congress ever since. He maintains close contacts throughout the active, reserve, and retired special operations communities. Previous relevant writings for the House Committee on Armed Services include *U.S. Special Operations Forces* (published commercially as *Green Berets, SEALs, and Spetsnaz*) and *U.S. Low-Intensity Conflict Experience, 1898-1990* (published commercially as *America's Small Wars: Lessons for the Future*).

ISBN 0-16-043191-3